The 4x4 BOOK

First published in May 2006

A catalogue record for this book is available from the British Library

ISBN 1 84425 304 X

Library of Congress catalog card no 2005935263

Published by Haynes Publishing, Sparkford, Yeovil, Somerset BA22 7JJ, UK

Tel: 01963 442030 Fax: 01963 440001
Int. tel: +44 1963 442030 Int. fax: +44 1963 440001
E-mail: sales@haynes.co.uk
Website: www.haynes.co.uk

Haynes North America Inc.,
861 Lawrence Drive, Newbury Park,
California 91320, USA

Designed by Richard Parsons

Printed and bound in Great Britain
by J. H. Haynes & Co. Ltd, Sparkford

Photograph Credits
All photographs and illustrations courtesy of the author except where credited otherwise.
Photograph appearing on pages 90–91 courtesy of Ifor Williams

WARNING
While every attempt has been made throughout this book to emphasise the safety aspects of working on a car, the publishers, the author and the distributors accept no liability whatsoever for any damage, injury or loss resulting from the use of this book. If you have any doubts about your ability to safely work on a car then it is recommended that you seek advice from a professional engineer.

Jurisdictions which have strict emission control laws may consider the running of certain vehicles or any modifications to a vehicle to be an infringement of those laws. You are advised to check with the appropriate body or authority whether your proposed purchase or modification complies fully with the law. The publishers accept no liability in this regard.

The 4x4 Book

The essential guide to buying, owning, enjoying and maintaining a 4x4

1
The 4x4
explosion

2
Living
with a 4x4

3
Running
a 4x4

7
The
crossovers

8
The
soft-roader

9
SUVs &
executives

Introduction

The market for new 4x4s has seen remarkable growth during the early years of the 21st century, a trend started way back in the 1980s when the notion of an all-wheel-drive vehicle being more than just an agricultural workhorse was first explored. These days, 4x4s are more popular than ever, as well as being both aspirational and trendsetting. The 4x4 has become one of the ultimate motoring fashion icons, although there's far more to the genre than that, as *The 4x4 Book* sets out to prove. So whether you're the first-time buyer of a 4x4 or you've been a convert for a number of years, you'll find plenty within these pages to entertain and inform.

Not everybody approves of the popularity of 4x4s, with anti-4x4 groups and protesters being high-profile in their criticisms. Again, this book attempts to set the record straight, as well as providing invaluable information for those about to enter the all-wheel-drive market for the first time.

What type of 4x4 will best suit your needs? How can you tell a crossover from an SUV? What do you need to know if you're thinking of heading off-road? What's the best advice if you've never towed with a 4x4 before? What are the extra cost implications of running a 4x4 compared with a conventional family car? What are the pros and cons of buying a Japanese 'grey' import? What's life like with a 4x4 day-to-day? And what information should you be armed with before venturing into the secondhand 4x4 market? These and many more questions will be answered within *The 4x4 Book*.

The 4x4 scene has never been bigger, with more newcomers getting involved every day. And, thanks to *The 4x4 Book*, there's now plenty of advice readily available for all. Have fun!

Acknowledgements

After such a long involvement in the 4x4 scene, including two separate periods as editor of a national 4x4 magazine, I have found it a real pleasure writing *The 4x4 Book*. I'm particularly grateful to Rowena Hoseason and Emm Walters – former and current editors respectively of *4x4 Mart* – for all their support.

Among the many other names I could mention, I'd like to thank Rod Jones for his unstinting encouragement and Frank Westworth for so much authorial inspiration over the years.

I am also indebted to Haynes Publishing's Mark Hughes, Steve Rendle and Christine Smith for their professional help and tremendous enthusiasm with this and all other projects.

Finally, to all the hard-working people in the various UK press offices that represent so many 4x4 manufacturers, a heartfelt thank you.

I hope you enjoy the 4x4 extravaganza that follows.

Paul Guinness
May 2006

OPPOSITE The Nissan Murano shows just how much 4x4 styling has evolved over the years *(Nissan)*

LEFT Whether you're the first-time buyer of a 4x4 or you've been a convert for many years, *The 4x4 Book* answers so many of the questions you've probably been wondering about *(Author)*

BELOW Family 4x4 or serious off-roader? There's now a wide choice of both *(Land Rover)*

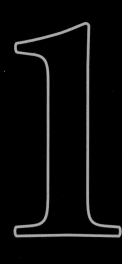

The 4x4 explosion

Shifting worlds

How things have changed in the world's car markets over the years. You don't have to go back too far, for example, to see that 4x4s were once the sole preserve of rural dwellers who needed the all-year-round capabilities that four-wheel drive provided. Nevertheless, the 4x4 scene isn't exactly a new phenomenon, for it was way back in 1948 that the original Land Rover first went into production, itself inspired by the all-American Willys Jeep that had performed so many admirable duties during World War II. But it wasn't until the early 1980s that the allure of driving a 4x4 began spreading into the towns and cities of most developed countries.

These days, of course, 4x4s are everywhere, with Americans in particular being enormous fans of the breed. Indeed, the best-selling vehicles in 21st-century America are 4x4s (or SUVs as they're more commonly known there) and pick-up trucks, with conventional cars and station wagons lagging behind in popularity. That means serious Stateside success for the world's most creative and innovative 4x4 manufacturers.

Europe – and the UK in particular – may not have embraced full-size SUVs in quite the same way as the USA, but there has still been a dramatic shift in the 4x4 market. It's true to say that 4x4s and SUVs (that's 'sports utility vehicles' by the way) have never been more popular than they are in modern-day Britain, as a quick glance at figures provided by the Society of Motor Manufacturers & Traders quickly testifies.

In 1995, sales of 4x4s and SUVs in the UK totalled 80,427; a healthy enough figure that represented 4.1 per cent of the entire market –

itself a major increase on ten years earlier. By 2004, though, that sales figure had more than doubled to an impressive 179,439 units and a significant 7 per cent of the market. For manufacturers of 4x4s the world over, such figures represent extra sales and profit.

So why did this dramatic change come about?

Partly because today's company car drivers and private buyers alike seem to appreciate something just a bit different from the norm. This has resulted in a truly fragmented car market, with manufacturers under increased pressure to offer what are perceived as niche models as well as more mainstream choices.

The days are gone when a car company could get away with producing just a supermini, a medium-size hatchback and a family saloon, with perhaps the odd estate car thrown in for good measure. These days, to be truly successful, manufacturers also need to offer three different sizes of MPV, a brace of sports cars or convertibles and, of course, a whole family of 4x4s. Not even a solo 4x4 offering will suffice, which is why most companies that have already entered this market now provide at least three different SUVs or 4x4s each.

Sometimes it feels as if they're all at it, with Japanese and Korean companies being particularly keen on spreading their 4x4 wings. At the time of writing, Honda offers both the HR-V and CR-V; Toyota does rather well with the RAV4, Land Cruiser and Land Cruiser Amazon; Nissan offers a range of five 4x4s in the shape of the X-Trail, Terrano II, Pathfinder, Munaro and Patrol; Mitsubishi enjoys success with the Shogun/Pajero Pinin, Shogun/Pajero Sport, Outlander and, of course, the Shogun/Pajero itself; Suzuki has plenty of followers of its Jimny and Grand Vitara models; Kia has the Sportage and the successful Sorento; and even Hyundai offers a three-vehicle choice in the shape of Tucson, Santa Fe and Terracan. That's before we even begin to look at what's available from European manufacturers.

Even those companies that don't currently have a 4x4 or SUV in their range are, in many cases, in the process of developing at least one, while other manufacturers are said to be seriously looking into the possibility. It's even become widely expected that SUVs bearing Jaguar and Bentley badges will be appearing at some stage – and why not? If Porsche can do

well with the Cayenne, Mercedes-Benz with the M-Class and Lexus with the RX300, the world obviously has no problems whatsoever with seeing an upmarket badge on a 4x4. The success of the most expensive versions of the Range Rover is proof of the upmarket potential of today's SUVs.

The popularity of the modern-day SUV and the general fragmentation of the world's car markets still need to be kept in perspective. Listen to some people – and especially to some campaign groups – and you could be forgiven for thinking the UK in particular was being taken over by 4x4s. Yet a glance at the official sales figures provided by the SMMT shows this plainly isn't true. The top ten list of best-sellers almost invariably includes such models as Ford's Fiesta and Focus, Vauxhall's Corsa and Astra, Peugeot's 206, Renault's Clio, Volkswagen's Golf and so on.

Don't forget that if 7 per cent of Britain's new car sales are made up of 4x4s and SUVs, then a whopping 93 per cent aren't. So let's keep a sense of perspective before panicking about 4x4s taking over the whole country, shall we? In any case, the vast majority of 4x4s and SUVs sold in the UK aren't the same petrol-guzzling monsters that we tend to associate with America. In fact, the most popular models on sale in Britain are also some of the most compact on the market.

BELOW The 4x4 market has made major inroads into the luxury car scene in the 21st century, with the all-wheel-drive Cayenne now being Porsche's best-selling vehicle *(Porsche)*

Busting
the myths

If the early years of the 21st century are synchronous with an increase in new 4x4 sales, they'll also be remembered for the reactions of the anti-4x4 camp and the protests that have been created as a result. Much of the controversy has centred around the use of 4x4s in urban areas and for the daily school run, and it's a subject on which many people appear to have an opinion. As ever, what could be a sensible and productive argument often declines into hysteria and hype.

It's perfectly true that the vast majority of parents who drive their children to school, or commuters who drive to work every day, don't actually need all-wheel drive to get them through. It's equally true, though, that most of the 4x4s sold for such purposes aren't actually V8-engined behemoths but are rather smaller, more economical and less polluting than that.

In April 2005, anti-4x4 protesters went as far as entering Land Rover's famous Solihull plant, successfully bringing to a halt production of the Range Rover for an entire day. Land Rover weren't impressed, given the loss of production and the negative publicity generated. But the protesters' biggest success, it could be argued, was in keeping the 4x4 debate alive.

To help redress the balance a little, Britain's weekly *Autocar* magazine entered the debate at the end of May 2005, with the magazine's deputy editor Chas Hallett stating: 'The vast majority of 4x4s sold in this country pump out no more CO_2, use no more fuel and, in fact, are no bigger than their lower-slung alternatives. Some are only guilty of being taller – but that also makes them more visible to the environmental lobby.

'The SUV is an important product for the motor industry, and a desirable one for consumers looking for versatility, towing ability, increased seating capacity and true go-anywhere capability. Consumers have the right to choose the vehicle of their choice and must not be intimidated by campaigners – especially when the facts they are using are out of date and misleading.'

Facts and figures

To back up such claims, *Autocar* decided to tackle individually the various accusations levelled at 4x4s and their owners, and it made for fascinating reading. Have a look through the following statements, reproduced here from *Autocar*'s press release of May 31st 2005, which managed to answer most 4x4 criticisms quite effectively and helped readers to retain a sense of perspective:

☒ 4x4s are unsafe

As a general rule, 4x4s protect occupants very well in a crash and, contrary to popular belief, they're no more dangerous to pedestrians than most ordinary hatchbacks. European testers Euro NCAP have certified the BMW X5, Volvo XC90 and VW Touareg as top-ranking five-star vehicles.

☒ There are more 4x4s in urban areas than elsewhere

Only 7.0 per cent of cars sold [in 2004] were 4x4s – 179,439 were registered … in a new car market of over 2.5 million cars. In London, only 3.5 per cent of privately registered cars are 4x4s.

☒ 4x4s are less economical than other cars

The prevalence of diesel engines makes many 4x4s no more thirsty than a typical family car. The Land Rover Freelander Td4 diesel, one of the UK's most popular 4x4s, returns an average 37.2mpg – identical to that of a Ford Mondeo 1.8 petrol.

☒ 4x4s pollute more than other cars

CO_2 levels from 4x4s have dropped by 14.6 per cent since 1997, and a Volvo XC90 D5 4x4 now produces less than the maker's 2.4-litre V50 estate. Emission-free 4x4s will soon appear on the roads – Lexus has just launched a hybrid RX400 which has both a traditional petrol engine and two powerful electric motors.

☒ 4x4s are bigger than other cars

In relation to the amount of road space they take up, 4x4s are comfortably overshadowed by big luxury saloons. They are taller than average, and as such harder to see around in traffic, but even in this respect they're not the worst offenders. Citroën's Berlingo mini-MPV, for example, is taller than a BMW X5.

What's the attraction?

But why is it that increasing numbers of buyers of new and used cars are turning to the 4x4 scene every year, looking for something a bit different in their next vehicle? Well, perhaps that's exactly what most of the appeal is: the opportunity to drive something that's just a tad more interesting than the average four-door saloon or five-door hatchback. To be honest, the reasons why people choose to drive 4x4s are as many and varied as the 4x4s themselves.

There's been a suggestion that much of the appeal can be attributed to snobbery, and there may be more than a grain of truth in this. Owners of the biggest, most opulent 4x4s on offer are often accused of 'lording it' over drivers of smaller, less expensive cars. Understandably, that can be annoying to many people, but don't forget the point I made earlier that the most upmarket 4x4s are the ones that sell in the smallest numbers throughout Europe, so the reality is that it's a relatively rare experience.

Surely, however, snobbery can't be the reason why somebody would choose to drive a Land Rover Freelander or Toyota RAV4 rather than a Ford Focus or Vauxhall Astra? Well, possibly. After all, even relatively compact 4x4s like these are seen as aspirational and desirable these days. Yet in reality, most owners opt for them because they simply fit in with their lifestyles, and perhaps they also rather like the image that's portrayed as a result.

It's true that most 4x4s offer exactly what many families and other buyers are looking for nowadays. There's more space on board for people and belongings, while passengers and driver alike have a greater all-round view thanks to the cars' elevated stance. The imaginative and thoughtfully designed interiors of many 4x4s offer all the convenience (and cup holders!) that even the most demanding families could desire, while the greater towing abilities of the vehicles also make them more appealing (and more suited) to buyers with caravans, boats, trailers and horseboxes to haul around.

As for the issue of all-wheel traction, particularly for urban users … well, it is important to many buyers. It may be the case that most people spending their own money on a new or used SUV won't be inclined to go off-roading every weekend, but they like to know that, if the need or desire arose, their vehicles would be

capable of doing just that; and on the odd occasion that they have to drag a caravan across a sodden field, drive up a remote track during their break in the Scottish Highlands or deal with a minor snowdrift during the winter months, their 4x4s will tackle such tasks with aplomb.

OPPOSITE To be successful now, manufacturers need to have at least a couple of 4x4 offerings in their model ranges, hence the existence of Honda's HR-V (shown here) and CR-V models *(Honda)*

LEFT The reality of 4x4s around town, though, is that most of them are compact designs that take up no more road area than a standard family car *(Mitsubishi)*

BELOW Even a fairly compact 4x4 has huge practical advantages over the average hatchback, ideal for owners who enjoy outdoor leisure pursuits *(Toyota)*

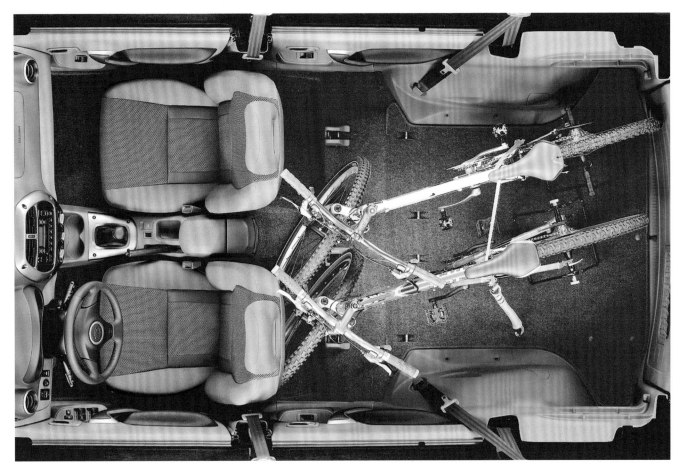

Jumping on board

Let's assume then, that you've decided to join the world of 4x4 ownership. What exactly can you expect from your experience – and are there likely to be many pitfalls along the way?

The issues of living with and running a 4x4 will be dealt with in chapters two and three, which is where we'll compare various costs and determine how the driving and ownership experiences contrast with those of conventional cars. As for which models are available and which might best suit your needs, this will be covered between chapters seven and ten. Meanwhile, what's likely to happen once you've decided to jump on board and join the 4x4 scene?

In the vast majority of cases, you can expect the obvious advantages of all-wheel traction – unless you've bought one of those rare-in-the-UK SUVs that comes solely with two-wheel drive, such as the entry-level models in the Honda HR-V and

Hyundai Tucson ranges. Most HR-V and Tucson buyers do opt for four-wheel drive when ordering, but it's worth checking this before hastily snapping up a used example, only to find it's not actually a 4x4!

Once you've got the 4x4 of your choice, you may well start wondering how you ever managed without one. All-wheel traction can come into its own in all sorts of situations, and not just for those who decide to go off-roading at official Off-Road Fun Days every weekend. You'll also find it handy when holidaying, when towing and even when dealing with atrocious winter weather conditions. Whether your SUV offers part-time or full-time four-wheel drive, that extra traction will prove invaluable at some point during your ownership.

Of course, if you want to take things further and embark upon a spot of 'proper' off-roading, there are plenty of suggestions to be found in chapter five. The great news is that such activity can be enjoyed even if your total budget for both the vehicle and any modifications is downright tiny.

For those owners who simply want everyday transport from their 4x4, the advantages are significant. The internal height difference between, say, a Land Rover Freelander and a Ford Focus Estate means far more convenience when trying to squeeze on board all the family's paraphernalia. The fact that most 4x4s offer stronger, more robust suspension than, for example, a conventional estate car also brings advantages when towing heavy trailers as it will usually mean less strain and long-term damage, and greater overall reliability.

There are downsides, of course. Many 4x4s suffer far poorer ride quality than the best traditional cars, a result of the compromise between off-road competence and on-road comfort. This means that long journeys can often be more tiresome and less enjoyable. Yet there are many 4x4s that manage to get the compromise pretty much spot-on, and I'll be taking a look at the best of these further on in the book.

Whatever your reasons for being attracted to 4x4 ownership – style, looks, image, toughness, good-old-fashioned off-road capability or simple all-round convenience – there is sure to be a model on today's new and used markets that will suit you. So whether you've just bought your very first 4x4, you've yet to buy one at all or you've owned more over the years than you can remember, you're part of a growing and very enthusiastic clan. By the time you get to the end of this book, you should have a much greater understanding of the issues than when you started.

OPPOSITE Towing a heavy trailer both on- and off-road is made a lot easier with a robust 4x4 and the obvious advantages of all-wheel traction *(Isuzu)*

BELOW Tackling winter weather conditions? Even if you never venture off-road, four-wheel drive has major all-year-round advantages *(Kia)*

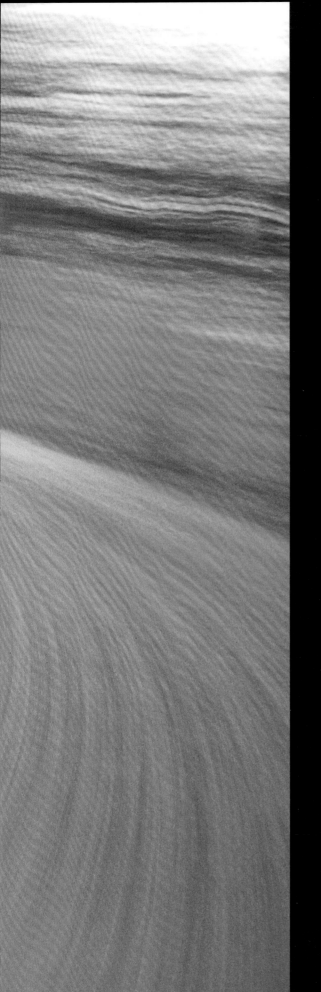

Living
with a 4x4

A question
of budget

Like so many other motorists, you find yourself tempted by the prospect of owning (or running) a 4x4. You like the style, the image, the capabilities and all the other advantages on offer – but you need to be sure you're not about to make a major mistake. How can you be certain that a 4x4 will actually be the ideal vehicle for you? It's advisable to double check your requirements and your expectations before jumping into the 4x4 scene, because a lack of research could bring a host of unpleasant surprises at a later date.

The good news about today's 4x4 market is that it's packed full of new and used vehicles just waiting to be snapped up – almost irrespective of the budget you have available. So whether you're intent on spending the minimum on a secondhand vehicle or breaking the bank with a spanking-new all-wheel-drive machine, there really is plenty of choice available.

At the very bottom end (price-wise) of the 4x4 market, you could find yourself an ancient and extremely basic Suzuki SJ, a tiny runabout with surprisingly effective off-road capabilities. But, perhaps inevitably, it's not a vehicle that will suit everyone, its lack of performance and complete absence of refinement ensuring its

OPPOSITE A pre-Defender coil-sprung Land Rover 90 makes a superb and straightforward off-road machine, although its fairly agricultural on-road feel is the compromise (Author)

LEFT No matter how minuscule the budget, just about everyone can afford to buy and run a 4x4 – even if it's an elderly model that has already seen plenty of use (Author)

appeal is limited mainly to the off-road fraternity these days.

The reason for mentioning the good-old Suzuki SJ was to point out just how little can be spent buying a usable and practical 4x4 – and to emphasise how easy it is to buy a vehicle that's really not ideal for your needs. Yes, Suzuki's elderly offering is spectacular value for money in the 21st century; but if you place a high value on such areas as occupant safety, on-road handling, performance and prestige, it most certainly is not the vehicle for you. It may be an extreme example of how to end up with a 4x4 that doesn't really suit your needs, but it's a useful illustration – and it's just as applicable when you look at other sectors of the market.

Whatever your budget, you'll almost certainly find a vast array of different makes and models of 4x4s available to you. Even with a modest sum of money burning a hole in your bank account, you can treat yourself to something compact and fairly economical to run (such as a Suzuki Vitara or Daihatsu Sportrak) or something far larger and much more expensive to keep on the road (for example, a Range Rover or a Mitsubishi Pajero V6). All four options will be fairly aged, will have covered a hefty mileage and almost certainly won't be in pristine condition. But at least you have those choices available.

The trouble is, having a wide choice of makes and models available to you, however much or little you're intending to spend, can bring its own array of dangers.

LEFT Need something larger? Elderly models such as this first-generation Mitsubishi Pajero long-wheelbase provide lots of space for those on a tight budget (Author)

Behind the **wheel**

Astonishingly, there are some first-time buyers of new and used 4x4s in this world who decide which model they want before they even get to sit in the driver's seat. They're the ones who are in the most danger of ending up with something wholly unsuitable. So, although it sounds like rather basic advice, do make sure you acquaint yourself with a particular model – and make sure you take a few extended test drives – before you make your final decision. That means you won't be buying the very first example you come across (almost always a bad move, in my experience), and you'll be more familiar with the driving style of more than one before you hand over any cash.

It's even more important for first-time owners of 4x4s to get behind the wheel than it is for those buyers already familiar with the genre, because, in driving style alone, there are some major differences between most 4x4s/SUVs and the average family saloon. It all starts as soon as you clamber aboard.

Notice the first difference? Yes, it's the obviously higher-up seating position that appeals to so many 4x4 owners. And it can be a positive boon, giving you and your passengers fantastic all-round views as well as a 'safe and secure' feeling. But it can have its drawbacks too, particularly when it comes to the difficulty of getting small children and elderly relatives on board. Think of this before you buy, and make sure you consider your own lifestyle needs before assuming that higher is automatically better.

The raised ride height that is such a trademark of the 4x4 and SUV classes also has implications when it comes to driving style – and particularly the all-important subject of handling and roadholding.

There are, of course, all-wheel-drive machines that have been created specifically to offer the ultimate in handling and grip on both road and track, with the Subaru Impreza Turbo and Ford Escort Cosworth models of the 1990s springing immediately to mind as obvious examples. Both are uncompromising road cars with about as much off-road talent as an electric toaster, and both offer the kind of grip that owners of lesser machinery still find astounding when they experience it for the first time.

But the 4x4/SUV scene is very different indeed. Here we have all-wheel-drive machines developed in most cases for some sort of off-road action, which invariably means an increased ride height, greater suspension travel, an emphasis on low-down torque and a completely different set of road manners.

The challenge facing most 4x4s and SUVs these days is to offer the ideal compromise between useful off-road competence and acceptable levels of on-road handling, roadholding and refinement. It's a compromise that has traditionally been very tricky to get right. Those 4x4s that have generally been the finest off-road have often lagged behind others when it comes to on-road behaviour; and those which have been the most highly praised for their on-

tarmac characteristics have sometimes been less than competent in the rough.

As technology has improved, so the compromise has become that bit easier to achieve, and today's new SUVs manage what would have been almost unthinkable twenty or thirty years ago. The original Land Rover Discovery of 1989, for example, was highly praised at its launch for offering class-leading levels of off-road capability. Even in completely unmodified form, a Discovery could take on just about any off-road situation and deal with it in a way that made rival companies green with envy. But the downside was the kind of roly-poly handling that made thousands of families feel travel sick on even the shortest

OPPOSITE The elevated driving position of most 4x4s and SUVs gives great all-round vision, but have you considered the disadvantages, too? *(Author)*

LEFT If you've never owned a 4x4 before, don't automatically assume you'll enjoy the driving experience. Take an extended test drive before making your decision *(Nissan)*

BELOW All-wheel-drive models such as the Subaru Impreza Turbo were developed for on-road grip rather than any kind of off-road capability. Obvious, isn't it? *(Author)*

journeys, combined with a ride quality that was at best mediocre. The Discovery excelled when it came to Land Rover's traditional off-road appeal, but was an obvious compromise in other respects.

Compare that with the Discovery 3 model of 15 years later and you'll appreciate how far companies such as Land Rover have come in terms of getting the on- and off-road compromise just about right. But, as ever, there's a downside: on-road behaviour is better than ever, but a number of models are now less impressive off-road than some of their predecessors. Or, if off-road prowess has indeed been maintained, it's often through over-complicated technology which, as today's models grow older and get passed on to their second or third owners, may cause long-term cost and reliability issues.

The average 4x4 of the 1980s and 1990s made use of a separate steel chassis rather than a car-like monocoque construction, which meant

ABOVE Even in unmodified form, the Series I Land Rover Discovery was a formidable off-roader. On-road, though, its cornering was less than perfect *(Frank Westworth)*

BELOW The Discovery 3 proves how today's models have successfully bridged the great on-road/off-road divide. It's superb in just about any setting *(Land Rover)*

less flexing and twisting of the bodyshell in extreme off-road conditions. It also tended to come with a basic but effective dual-range transfer box, and often a locking differential or two for good measure. It was all quite straightforward but immensely effective out in the rough. When it came to durability and expense, the simplicity of design brought obvious benefits there, too.

But a separate chassis in a 4x4 invariably means poorer on-tarmac ride quality and a more agricultural feel, which is why even the most traditional manufacturers of off-road machinery are now going the monocoque 'all-in-one' route. Prior to 2005, for example, Suzuki had stuck resolutely with the principle of a separate sturdy chassis for all its 4x4 models, but the announcement of an all-new Grand Vitara range that year saw the introduction of monocoque construction for the first time. It was all in an attempt to put the model on an equal footing with the Toyota RAV4 in terms of handling, roadholding and driver appeal, a strategy that worked – even if it did leave traditionalists and the off-road fraternity feeling a bit left out.

It's a not dissimilar situation at Land Rover, with examples of the (1989–97) Series I Discovery now being available to budget-conscious serious off-road enthusiasts who want to invest in some cost-effective modifications and have plenty of fun out in the rough. Both the vehicle and any desired upgrades are highly affordable, while the simplicity of its technology ensures it's capable of hard work and – should anything go wrong – is straightforward enough to repair. But will the

off-road fraternity be saying the same about 2004's monocoque-designed, technologically advanced Discovery 3 model by, say, 2015? Almost certainly not, for the technological complication of creating a class-leading luxury off-roader these days brings obvious implications for owners further down the line, whose priorities will be very different from those of the first owner.

The reason for pointing all this out now is to illustrate how important it is to prioritise your needs and expectations, particularly if you're the first-time buyer of a 4x4. Is off-road competence more important to you than on-road comfort and refinement? You need to decide, because your final choice of vehicle could vary hugely depending on your answer. Don't worry about this, because further on in the book we'll be looking at many specific models and outlining their various benefits and drawbacks – so as long as you know what you want and need from a vehicle, chapters seven to eleven will bring plenty of suggestions and ideas.

LEFT While the original Suzuki Grand Vitara of 1998–2005 used a separate steel chassis for structural rigidity when off-roading… *(Author)*

ABOVE …its successor employs a monocoque design. The result is greater on-road refinement, although off-road fanatics might not approve of such 'progress' *(Suzuki)*

Day to **day**

Even a top-handling 4x4 like a Toyota RAV4 will never go round corners in quite the same roll-free, ultra-grippy way as today's leading hot hatches, although most owners will be more than happy with the former's overall driving style. However, it's not just a 4x4's handling, roadholding and refinement that differ from more conventional cars – there's also the question of day-to-day living with a 4x4, its overall convenience and how it will actually fit into your life.

As outlined in Chapter One, there has been a lot of anti-4x4 reporting during the early years of the 21st century, much of the criticism coming from the assumption that all 4x4s are big, cumbersome and a sheer nuisance. In reality, of course, the best-selling 4x4s in the UK during that time (Land Rover Freelander, Toyota RAV4 and Honda CR-V) took up no more ground area than a medium-sized saloon or hatchback, which means that their contribution towards the congestion problem is no greater than that of most of the best-selling family cars that can be bought for similar money.

Even so, it still pays to check in detail the exact measurements of the new or used 4x4 you're thinking of buying – before you actually hand over your money. A secondhand 2000-model Land Rover Freelander Station Wagon, for example, measures 173 inches in overall length, which compares favourably with the 175-inch length of a Ford Focus Estate from the same year. Both models are therefore similar in terms of their contribution towards urban congestion.

But – and it's an important but – the Freelander comes in three inches wider than the Focus (including both models' door mirrors) and is a full twelve inches taller. When it comes to squeezing your family's mode of transport into a small garage, a carport or through a less-than-generous height-restricting barrier, such differences can be crucial. Take this into account when thinking about the all-round convenience of your particular choice.

Neither should you ignore such issues as the turning circle and overall manoeuvrability of 'your' 4x4 as compared with those of the conventional car you're also considering buying. If much of your driving is through the urban jungle, this may well be important to you. Once more, it comes down to an accurate and honest assessment of your needs, expectations and priorities before you make any decision.

OPPOSITE The Toyota RAV4 is one of the best-handling on-road machines in today's used 4x4 market – and is still one of the most popular buys throughout Europe *(Toyota)*

BELOW Do make sure the 4x4 you choose will fit into your life. Did you know this Freelander is twelve inches taller than a Ford Focus Estate of the same age? *(Land Rover)*

ABOVE If your used 4x4 is for urban use, check out its manoevrability during your test drive *(Author)*

Petrol versus **diesel**

Most of today's 4x4s and SUVs come with a choice of petrol or diesel power, and it's another dilemma that has seen a major shift in buying habits over the years – throughout Europe, but particularly in the UK. That's because modern diesel-powered cars enjoy a larger slice of the market than ever before, which has been reflected in the buying habits of 4x4 fans, too.

It's understandable why this should have happened. Diesels have always been more economical than their petrol equivalents, the downside being that they were traditionally noisy, smelly and lethargically slow. But a new wave of diesel developments during the 1990s (and continuing in the 21st century), led by common-rail direct-injection technology, has brought diesel engines that are now more powerful, faster, quieter, less polluting, more economical and vastly more refined than ever before. It's no wonder so many buyers of new 4x4s are now going the diesel route.

Larger 4x4 have always sold best in diesel guise, with models such as the Series I and II

Land Rover Discovery, Mitsubishi Pajero/Shogun, Toyota Land Cruiser, Nissan Terrano II and Patrol, Isuzu Trooper and – in later years – the Range Rover all being most popular in oil-burning form. This is because their petrol-engined alternatives, almost invariably with large V6 or V8 powerplants providing the action, were prohibitively uneconomical and, as a result, often suffered fairly dire depreciation. But further down the 4x4 scale, particularly when going back to the 1980s, petrol power was all the rage – hence British buyers of the early Suzuki Vitara and Toyota RAV4 weren't even offered a diesel alternative.

Oh, how times change. All but the very tiniest 4x4s (such as the Daihatsu Terios and Suzuki Jimny) now come in both petrol and diesel versions in most European markets, and it's the latter offerings that are rapidly growing in popularity. Thanks to all that new technology, the power and performance penalty of driving a diesel is often minuscule.

Although bigger 4x4s have always sold well in diesel guise, drivers had to get used to making a major performance sacrifice along the way. In 1991, for example, the UK-spec Mitsubishi Shogun five-door turbo diesel had to make do with a mere 98bhp from its 2.5-litre powerplant, compared with a far healthier 147bhp from its 3.0-litre V6-engined petrol alternative. This gave respective top speeds of 88mph and 103mph, which guaranteed a much more lethargic driving

style for the TD derivative. By 2005, though, the latest-spec Shogun range was featuring 3.2-litre direct-injection turbo-diesel versions with 158bhp on tap – a healthy improvement and a great illustration of just how far diesel technology had developed during that decade-and-a-half.

Not only are today's diesel-powered 4x4s a joy to own and drive compared with their predecessors, they're still impressively economical up against their petrol equivalents. Taking the 2005-model Toyota RAV4 as an example, there was a choice of a 2.0-litre petrol engine or a similar-capacity direct-injection turbo diesel that year, offering outputs of 147bhp and 114bhp respectively. That may sound like quite a difference, but it equated to a mere 6mph gap in top speeds and just a 1.3-second time lag in the 0–60mph sprint, but where the turbo diesel really

ABOVE Today's diesel-powered 4x4s are better than ever, with seriously improved refinement and performance from just about all of them *(Hyundai)*

OPPOSITE At the start of the 1990s, the poor old Mitsubishi Shogun/Pajero 2.5 TD had to make do with a mere 98bhp, resulting in rather leisurely on-road performance *(Author)*

BELOW By 2005, the equivalent turbo-diesel Shogun/Pajero was churning out 158bhp, thanks to its 3.2-litre direct-injection powerplant *(Mitsubishi)*

scored was in its official 'combined' fuel consumption figure of 39.8mpg compared with just 32.5mpg for the petrol version. For anybody driving, say, 15,000 miles per year, that difference meant an extra 84 gallons of fuel used in a twelve-month period, or an extra 253 gallons over three years.

You can work out the cost implications of that yourself, depending on fluctuations in fuel prices at the time of reading, and you might be tempted to think 'Well, it's not a huge difference in total, so is it really worth opting for a diesel?'. But consider this: as long as diesel-powered 4x4s remain so popular, they are likely to enjoy greater residuals than their petrol equivalents – and with depreciation being one of today's biggest motoring expenses, that brings a significant saving during the first few years of ownership. It's not just an issue of fuel consumption we're talking about here.

Before moving on from fuel economy altogether, let's take a quick look at how it can vary between a 4x4 and a similar-engined conventional car, as this can come as something of a shock to an unsuspecting first-time buyer.

ABOVE Larger models – such as the early Nissan Terrano II range – have always sold best in diesel guise, not least because of the drastic difference in fuel consumption *(Author)*

BELOW There are now diesel-powered versions of most 4x4s readily available, the pre-2006 Daihatsu Terios being one of the few available solely in petrol-engined guise at the time of writing *(Daihatsu)*

Thanks to the extra weight, poorer aerodynamics and extra driveline drag of a 4x4 or SUV compared with the average family saloon or hatchback, fuel economy can suffer – and it's something you should research yourself once you've decided on the make and model of 4x4 that tempts you. Official figures are readily available in most of the monthly motoring magazines aimed at buyers of new and used vehicles, so the process itself is simple – even if the results can be surprising.

Take the 1.8-litre petrol-engined Land Rover five-door Freelander as an example, a vehicle with an official 'combined' fuel consumption figure (gained from averaging the results for both the 'urban' cycle and 'extra urban') of just 27.3mpg compared with 36.2mpg for a 2005-model Vauxhall Astra 1.8 Estate. Over a period of twelve months and 12,000 miles, that adds up to an extra 108 gallons of fuel being used by the Freelander driver.

Most 4x4 drivers are happy to pay such a penalty for the pleasure of owning such a useful and impressive all-wheel-drive machine as a Freelander – or just about any other 4x4 for that matter. But it's something that every buyer should be aware of before they take delivery, particularly in such a country as the UK with its notoriously high levels of fuel taxation.

In much the same way that driving a 4x4 is a different experience from piloting a typical family saloon or hatchback, it seems the costs involved can vary, too – and we'll look at more of these in detail in chapter three. Meanwhile, take a long, hard look at your own requirements and what you expect from life with a 4x4. There will be a make and model available that suits you perfectly; but failing to make the ideal choice could be an expensive mistake and a sobering experience.

Running a 4x4

Paying for the privilege?

As well as the different driving characteristics and various ownership issues associated with 4x4s and outlined in the previous chapter, a number of cost implications come into play when you're considering entering the 4x4 scene for the first time – and that's equally true whether you're thinking of buying a new or used vehicle.

Such implications start with the very price you're paying for your 4x4 compared with a more conventional car of similar size, power and equipment levels. And the difference is particularly noticeable when opting for a brand new vehicle.

As a point of reference, let's look back to 2005 and some of the most popular 4x4s that were available brand new. One of the best sellers in the UK at that time was the Honda CR-V, with the sought-after 2.0 i-VTEC SE engine, giving you a well-equipped five-door vehicle with a healthy 147bhp.

To get the same kind of power and convenience from a similarly sized conventional car, spending slightly less than you would have done on the CR-V could have bought you a 142bhp Ford Focus 2.0 Zetec Estate – and you'd have ended up with a faster, more economical, better-handling family car as a result, as well as saving yourself a useful few pounds in the process. But to look at such on-paper facts in isolation is to miss the point.

Taking another example, again from 2005, British fans of the BMW brand could have spent a very hefty sum on an X5 4.4i V8 SE, an impressive all-wheel-drive leviathan with 320bhp on tap. Yet for around 12% less, they could instead have had the superb 545i SE – one of the world's greatest saloons, with 328bhp and superb driving characteristics to match.

So why was it that in two quite disparate sectors of the new-car market, a significant proportion of buyers opted for a more expensive, slower, less economical SUV rather than a more conventional-looking saloon or estate? Perhaps it comes back to the perception of buyers wanting to be seen in something different and a tad more interesting, as suggested in chapter one. But despite the obvious on-paper disadvantages of going the 4x4 route, there is one major area in which the all-wheel-drive SUV almost invariably scores: residuals.

Going back to our Honda CR-V versus Ford Focus example cited above, this is particularly interesting. According to Britain's *Car* magazine (August 2005), the Focus Estate we chose would still be worth around 40 per cent of its new value as a trade-in after three years and 36,000 miles. By comparison, the Honda CR-V we went for would apparently be worth around 55 per cent of its original cost, at the same age and mileage.

In the case of the two BMWs we mentioned, it's a not dissimilar story. After three years (at an average mileage of 12,000 per annum) the 545i SE would have residuals of approximately 46% as a trade-in, according to *Car* magazine. But the BMW X5 4.4i V8 SE trounced such figures with claimed residuals of just over 54 per cent after the same three years. You might have spent more buying the brand new X5 compared with its 5-Series rival, but the long-term ownership costs more than made up for this.

Well, almost. Before we all get excited at the prospect of a 4x4 being one of the best new-car investments on the market, there are two more facts to bear in mind.

Firstly, you are far more likely to get a healthy discount off the price of a conventional family car than you are from one of the more popular SUVs – and that's particularly true with our Honda CR-V

versus Ford Focus comparison. Few (if any) drivers of a Focus 2.0 Zetec Estate will have paid anywhere near its official list price when they took delivery – and this means its on-paper depreciation figure won't be quite as shocking in practice.

And secondly, we need to keep a careful eye on what's happening with new 4x4 sales before we can accurately predict true residuals for several years down the line. As new 4x4 and SUV sales increase, so secondhand supply will eventually begin to catch up with demand. Will 4x4s still represent such good depreciation-busting buys in years to come? Only time will tell. Happily, it seems that as demand for new 4x4s continues to build, so does demand on the secondhand market – and that means the situation should remain fairly stable (and predictable) for the foreseeable future.

The secondhand saga

It's an irony of the world's car markets that if a brand new vehicle holds its value exceptionally well (much to the delight of those buyers who chose it in the first place), the downside is that anybody seeking out a secondhand example will end up paying more for the privilege. So that's why, in just about every sector of Europe's secondhand 4x4 market, it's the SUVs that are priced higher than their conventional rivals of similar age, mileage and specification.

This seems to apply whether you're interested in buying a fifteen-year-old Suzuki Vitara, a six-year-old Land Rover Freelander or a twelve-month-old Toyota RAV4. Compare each one with just about any traditional saloon, hatchback or estate that cost roughly similar money when new and you'll find it's the 4x4 that is priced considerably higher.

Consequently, if you have a set budget in mind for your first (or next) secondhand 4x4, you'll find it buying you a far older vehicle than if you were in the market for an ordinary family car. But that needn't be a problem; there are thousands of buyers who would rather spend their hard-earned money on a well-preserved old Freelander than on a far newer family hatch – and who can blame them?

Service
charge

If buying a new or used 4x4 can be more expensive than buying a normal family car, what about the other costs involved during your period of ownership – including servicing and maintenance, fuel consumption, parts prices and so on? Happily, most of the mainstream 4x4s available for sensible money are also sensibly priced when it comes to maintenance – but there are still one or two areas that need bearing in mind.

By their very nature, 4x4s and SUVs tend to be more complicated machines than their conventional competitors, which can have an obvious knock-on effect on repair bills as they get older. This is why it is essential to ensure (once you've decided on the make and model of 4x4 in which you intend investing) that you buy the best, lowest-mileage example of its type. Remember, even those makes and models with the very best reputation for reliability will need some kind of unexpected attention as the miles mount and the years pass by.

It's also worth bearing in mind that the last few years have seen useful increases in the service intervals of most new vehicles, with many of today's 4x4s and SUVs requiring services at around 15,000-mile intervals (in the case of certain petrol-engined models) compared with 8000–10,000 mile intervals for their predecessors.

Similarly, it's not that long ago (specifically, back in the early 1980s) when a diesel-engined 4x4 would need a visit to the dealership every 3000–6000 miles for a service, an exercise that added a fair chunk to overall running costs over a period of several years. Again, thanks to massive improvements in diesel technology since the end of the 1990s, today's oil-burning 4x4s need no more regular attention than their mainstream counterparts, and this helps significantly.

Remember such changes when buying any used 4x4, and always investigate the service intervals recommended for the specific make and model of your choice. If you're intending to keep the vehicle for a few years, it's a cost that you'll need to factor in when doing your sums.

Fortunately, most of the 4x4s of the last twenty years or so are relatively straightforward, even if the existence of an all-wheel-drive set-up means – by definition – extra complication compared with a standard front- or rear-wheel-drive saloon or

hatchback. Most 4x4s, for example, use engines borrowed from elsewhere within their respective manufacturer's ranges, which brings obvious economies of scale for the car companies and relative ease of maintenance for 4x4 owners.

Britain's best-selling 4x4 from the late 1990s was the original-style Land Rover Freelander, base versions of which were fitted with the same 1.8-litre, 118bhp K-series petrol engine used elsewhere within what was then the Rover Group.

OPPOSITE As the miles mount, so things are more likely to go wrong – even on the most reliable of 4x4s. Try to buy the youngest, lowest-mileage example your budget will stretch to *(Author)*

LEFT So many 4x4s use engines borrowed from other vehicles. Shown here is the Freelander's 1.8-litre K-series unit, which also saw service in many Rovers and MGs over the years *(Author)*

BELOW Older 4x4s – and particularly diesels – require servicing at far more regular intervals than today's newcomers. Bear this in mind when calculating running costs *(Author)*

RIGHT Most 4x4s use engines and major componentry from elsewhere in their manufacturer's line-up *(Honda)*

OPPOSITE Off-road equipment, such as a dual-range transfer box, locking diffs or hill descent control, means a more complex make-up for most ageing 4x4s compared with their conventional opposition *(Author)*

As a result, the Freelander shares the same powerplant as various Rover 25s and 45s, with all the advantages (and one or two disadvantages, such as a tendency for early head-gasket failure in many instances) such sharing brings.

Yet that doesn't mean the Freelander cost exactly the same to have serviced as any regular Rover 25 might have done, for the extra complications of the 4x4's permanent all-wheel drive, dual-range transfer box, hill descent control,

BELOW Maintaining your 4x4's service history – even with elderly models – is an essential aid to future resale and will help to reassure potential buyers *(Author)*

ABS brakes and other such bonuses inevitably meant extra work, maintenance and expense as the miles mounted.

To make sure you're prepared for any such expenses, it's essential you carry out some research before you take the plunge into 4x4 ownership. It would obviously be too complicated (and far too dull) to list all the recommended service intervals and the likely costs for every popular 4x4 within this book. And, by the very nature of book publishing, such information would inevitably become dated. So the simple moral of this tale is to make sure you talk to whoever is likely to be maintaining your 4x4 before you actually make the purchase.

Will you be using a franchised main dealer, for example? If so, talk to them about any fixed-price servicing they may offer for certain models. Even if the dealership doesn't offer menu-style servicing, it should be able to give a clear idea of the kind of expense likely to be involved – and at what intervals. They will also advise on the recommended age and mileage for changing your 4x4's cam belt (an essential job if you're to avoid serious expense and catastrophic engine failure through neglect), as well as any other major jobs that need attending to at specific mileages.

If you're likely to be using a local garage for your servicing and repair needs, they should also be able to give an idea of the kind of regular costs involved in your specific make and model. Again, talk to them about the mileage you're likely to be covering and how often your vehicle is likely to need attention. Most independent garages offering a first-class service will be happy to advise on such matters if they're likely to be getting some work from you at a later date.

Finally, still on the subject of servicing, don't forget to maintain your vehicle's service history – no matter what its age or mileage. While I always recommend buying a 4x4 with a full service history, it's quite likely there will be a few gaps when it comes to far older vehicles; but that doesn't mean it's not worth keeping a full and complete record of all the work you have done during your period of ownership, as it will surely impress any prospective purchaser when the time comes to sell.

So whether your 4x4's history is complete or patchy at present, and irrespective of whether you'll be using a main dealer or an independent garage for your servicing and repairs, having those extra stamps in your service book and a clear and accurate record of what's been done (and when) is essential – both for your own peace of mind and for the future resale of your 4x4.

Spares and **parts**

A major advantage of today's booming 4x4 scene throughout Europe is the sheer number of off-road and 4x4 specialists able to help with the supply of spare parts and accessories. This often means items being available for significantly less than you would expect to pay from a main dealer. Over the years, there have been various issues arising over 4x4 spares, particularly in the UK, partly as a result of increasing numbers of grey imports being shipped over from Japan.

These days, grey imports are big business – which means scores of dealers within the scene importing and retailing the actual vehicles, as well as many more specialists focusing on spare parts and accessories for grey 4x4s. It's an area of the market in which even the manufacturers and official importers have become involved.

Take Mitsubishi, for example. There was a time when the British importers of the marque refused to supply parts for Pajeros (and other models) brought to the UK as secondhand grey imports. The company evidently thought that if it refused to condone grey Pajeros and was equally reluctant to offer parts for them, it would deter large numbers of buyers from deserting the UK-spec Shogun.

But it was a philosophy that failed, for innovative 4x4 specialists keen for a slice of the grey market started bringing in their own supplies of Japanese-spec Pajero spares, satisfying a rapidly expanding market and cashing in as a result. The upshot was a boom in sales of grey Pajeros, with unofficially imported examples eventually outnumbering official Shoguns on Britain's roads. This led to a reversal in Mitsubishi's attitude and, keen not to lose any more sales of spares to independent specialists, it began selling Pajero parts through its official dealer network.

The reason for mentioning this here is to point out that almost irrespective of the make and model of 4x4 you end up owning, you will find an often surprising range of parts and accessories available for it via your nearest franchised dealer – even if it's a model not officially imported into your country. Just as importantly, you have a far greater choice available to you.

Whether it's a British Land Rover, an all-American Jeep, a Japanese Toyota or a Korean-built Kia that takes your fancy, you'll find there are plenty of 4x4 specialists throughout Europe – and particularly in the UK – able to offer competitively priced spare parts and add-ons. In fact, a quick glance at this book's appendix will give you an idea of just what a plethora of independent specialists there currently is, all of them claiming to offer advantages over their closest rivals.

Land Rover owners are especially well-blessed with specialists, though the Japanese 4x4 scene doesn't lag far behind. Such companies are particularly useful when it comes to upgrades and enhancements for your 4x4, with advice for off-road improvements always being readily available. Take a look at chapter eleven for more information on accessories, upgrades and add-ons – and then have a chat with a specialist in your particular marque before deciding just how far you want to take things.

So how do parts prices in general compare with more conventional machinery, such as the average family hatch or saloon? On the whole, pretty well. But, as ever, you need to apply plenty of common sense before you make any assumptions about the cost of spares.

For example, make sure you're comparing like with like. You can spend a fair amount of your hard-earned money on a well-used Toyota Land Cruiser full-size 4x4 or a one-owner-from-new Toyota Yaris supermini. But although they may cost the same to buy (albeit they'll be drastically different in age and mileage), the cost of running each will vary enormously, and you will certainly end up paying more for oil and air filters, brake pads, an exhaust system or a wheel bearing for a Land Cruiser than you ever would for a Yaris. The difference in size and design between two such vehicles guarantees this.

On the other hand, if you're comparing a 4x4 with a conventional car that can be seen as more of a genuine rival, you may be pleasantly surprised. If

you're in the market for a small hatchback, for example, you could spend a similar amount of cash on a Suzuki Jimny or Daihatsu Terios instead. And you'll generally find the cost of most service items and standard spare parts broadly similar between the two different genres of vehicle.

It's much the same story when you look further upmarket, too. A brand new Land Rover Discovery V8 HSE in 2005 would set you back by just about the same amount as would a Jaguar XJ8 Sport. Both are luxury vehicles, albeit one is a 4x4 and the other is a sleek and seductive saloon. As it happens, both should cost roughly similar sums to have serviced and repaired as the years pass, although the extra complication of the Discovery's all-wheel-drive set-up may add to the bills as the model eventually enters old age.

For owners of older vehicles, there's no shortage of specialist 4x4 breakers around, details of which appear in this book's appendix. Buying used parts from a breaker can make a lot of sense, as considerable sums of money can be saved compared with buying all-new items. But do be sensible about what you'd consider buying used, as you should never be tempted to fit secondhand items that have any kind of a safety implication. It's fine to replace damaged or rusty body panels with secondhand replacements from a breaker's yard, for example, but it would be foolhardy in the extreme to consider removing tyres, seat belts, brake parts or suspension components from a used vehicle that might have been in an accident or even drastically failed its MoT test. 4x4 breakers can be hugely useful resources for owners on a budget, but should never be used when to do so could risk the safety of you, your family and other road users.

OPPOSITE With many of today's more upmarket 4x4s – such as the Volkswagen Touareg – offering serious on-road performance, they need to be fitted with high-speed tyres to match, as described overleaf *(Volkswagen)*

BELOW By shopping around and using the services of specialists rather than franchised dealers, it's possible to save considerable sums when buying spares for your 4x4 *(Author)*

Rubber up!

If parts prices can be competitive for most mainstream 4x4s, the same doesn't necessarily apply to the subject of tyres – although much depends not just on the make and model of 4x4 that graces your driveway but also your intended usage of it. Many 4x4s that experience life only on tarmac, for example, are fitted with road-biased tyres that are little different in specification from what you'd find on any conventional car; but if the temptation is there to venture off-road (even just occasionally), you'll need something a bit more competent in the rough, which is where things can start to get a little complicated.

There is a huge assortment of different tyres on the market aimed at 4x4 owners, with such famous marques as BF Goodrich, General Tires, Pirelli, Michelin, Bronco, Goodyear and Bridgestone all well-represented on the 4x4 scene. Your final choice of make will come down to a compromise between your requirements and your budget, although it always pays to buy the very best tyres you can afford.

As with other sectors of the market, there are 4x4 tyres available (particularly from Eastern Europe) at what seem to be bargain prices. But many owners have reported premature wear compared with the better-known makes, as well as poorer grip when it's needed most. No matter what type of 4x4 you drive, irrespective of whether it's used mainly on- or off-road, opting for the very cheapest tyres on the market can be a false economy.

The type (rather than the make) of tyre you choose will depend entirely on your 4x4's intended usage, as well as the specification of the vehicle itself. Today's fastest 4x4s, for example, with big powerful petrol engines and a real emphasis on tarmac-only progress, will generally use high performance on-road tyres – essential for any vehicle with genuine performance potential. For most people, though, the choices tend to come down to all-season on-road tyres, standard on-road tyres, all-terrain tyres, mud-terrain tyres or – for very specialised usage – even sand tyres.

So how do you find the right tyre to suit your 4x4 and the way you use it? The best advice is to talk to some of the 4x4 specialist companies we've listed in this book's appendix and ask them what the ideal choice of tyre is for your make and model. Tell them how much of your driving is likely to be off-road, how important comfort is to you, and also what kind of a budget you have to play with. They'll then be able to come up with the ideal compromise for your needs. The perfect choice of tyre will vary between different 4x4s and different owners, so it's essential to get as much individual advice as possible.

It's particularly useful to log on to www.4site4x4.co.uk, a website which brings together companies specialising in 4x4 tyres for all makes and models. In the UK, find out where your nearest 4site retailer is and have a chat about what you're trying to achieve with your new tyres. You might be surprised at just how many options are on the market, at least one of which should be ideal for your needs and your particular vehicle.

Do remember that if you're tempted by the prospect of all-terrain rubber to transform your everyday 4x4 into a more competent off-road machine, you'll notice a serious deterioration in the vehicle's ride quality and comfort level, as well as new handling and roadholding characteristics.

For this reason, many owners who go off-roading at weekends have a spare set of steel wheels clad with off-road tyres tucked away in the garage or shed. That way they can continue to drive their 4x4 with on-road tyres fitted during the week, making the everyday experience a more comfortable affair. But when the need arises for a spot of off-road action, it's a simple enough task to swap the wheels for the off-road set – and away they go. It may sound a bit of a nuisance, but it's an excellent way of dealing with the on- and off-road compromise of any daily-use 4x4.

Whatever kind of 4x4 rubber you opt for, make sure they're good quality tyres that are correctly suited to your vehicle – and, as you should with any car, make sure the tyres on each axle match. Also, don't forget to inspect your tyres regularly for cuts and other damage caused by off-road driving; damage does occur and, if ignored, can pose a real threat to safety on the road.

OPPOSITE Using your normal road tyres in extreme off-road situations can create all kinds of problems *(Author)*

LEFT Even with four-wheel drive fully employed, the wrong kind of tyres on your 4x4 can make driving in mud… *(Author)*

LEFT…or even snow, a less than successful experience *(Author)*

BELOW Your choice of rubber is an essential part of your off-road enjoyment *(Author)*

Insurance issues

Finding appropriate insurance cover for your 4x4 needn't be any more complicated than insuring a conventional car, although there are a few points to bear in mind before you start shopping around.

RIGHT A Toyota Surf makes a sensible used buy – but check you can afford the insurance before you buy, as there's often an extra loading for grey imports *(Author)*

First of all, particularly if you're a first-time buyer, do be aware that insurance groupings can be higher for a 4x4 than for an ordinary car of similar value – and, if so, this will inevitably mean some extra expense. Anybody choosing to buy a Suzuki Jimny 1.3 JLX (rated at UK insurance group 7) instead of a similarly priced Ford Fiesta 1.25 16v Zetec (insurance group 3) will obviously find themselves experiencing higher quotes. Similarly, a Land Rover Freelander 2.0 Td4 finds itself in insurance group 13, whereas the similarly priced Ford Mondeo 2.0 DCi enjoys a group 9 rating. So if insurance is likely to be a major issue to you, it certainly pays to start your research and get a few quotes sorted out long before you actually invest in a 4x4.

Another point to be aware of is the importance of checking your insurance company's position concerning off-road driving, particularly when differentiating between private land and rights of way (green lanes). You don't necessarily need to have your vehicle insured when off-roading on private land, but you must be aware of the risks involved – and if any damage is caused to your vehicle, it will be up to you to pay for any repairs.

Whichever insurance company you choose to do business with, always make sure they're aware of any modifications you've carried out on your 4x4 – even if this simply includes a set of alloy wheels or some off-road tyres. Failure to make the insurer aware of every non-standard item could make any future insurance claims null and void. Don't take any chances.

Finally, what's the situation if you want to insure a grey 4x4 that has been imported secondhand from Japan? Fortunately, it's easier now than it's ever been, with most mainstream insurance companies willing to offer cover on grey Mitsubishi Pajeros, Isuzu Bighorns, Toyota Surfs and all the other popular imports. But there is a downside – and that means you'll find yourself paying anything between 25 per cent and 40 per cent extra compared with the cost of insuring a UK-spec vehicle.

Why does this extra expense exist? For a variety of reasons. Certain grey models, it seems, are statistically more likely to be stolen or involved in accidents than their UK-spec equivalents. (There's no obvious, logical reason for this – but since when did statistics take logic into account?) Many grey imports also tend to be better-

equipped and cosmetically more complicated, which means even a minor shunt can involve the replacement of more trim, trickier paint schemes and the like.

Whatever the make, model or specification of 4x4 you're trying to get insured, you'll find shopping around for quotes well worthwhile – but make sure you do this before you take the plunge and end up buying a 4x4 that you simply can't afford to insure. Also, don't forget to give some of today's specialist 4x4 insurers a try before automatically opting for one of the mainstream operators; you may find a policy more suited to your needs, particularly if your vehicle is non-standard or is an unusual model. Check out any 4x4 magazine to catch these specialist insurers' latest advertisements and special offers.

OPPOSITE If you're driving round in a modified 4x4, is your insurance company aware of the upgrades? Failure to inform them could make your policy null and void (*Author*)

LEFT Even at the bottom end of the 4x4 market, insurance for something as tiny as a Suzuki Jimny will work out dearer than for a Fiesta of similar value (*Suzuki*)

BELOW If you're thinking of buying a Japanese grey import, such as a Mitsubishi Pajero, you'll find most mainstream insurers willing to offer cover these days (*Author*)

Preparing for the MoT test

Motorists' dread of the annual MoT test (as with cars, compulsory on all 4x4s over three years of age in the UK) hasn't changed much over the years, even if the test itself is now drastically different from what it was when first introduced in the 1960s. Back then, as long as your car stopped and steered, it stood a reasonable chance of passing its test. Nowadays, inspectors are a bit more thorough. And, despite our moans and groans about the unfairness of it all, most of us would probably agree that a tightening up of the test was a good move towards public safety.

Relatively few vehicles pass their MoT tests first time every time, but you can increase the chances by spending less than a day getting your 4x4 ready. With the cost of the MoT test now at an all-time high, it's wise to be prepared. Admittedly, our procedure won't guarantee a pass, but it might make you aware of problem areas before you venture to the local MoT garage.

Firstly, a word about legalities: despite what some prophets of doom might tell you, it IS still legal for you to drive your car to its MoT test even if your old certificate has expired – as long as you have valid insurance cover, the MoT is pre-booked and you drive there by the quickest route (not via your favourite holiday destination). Make sure your MoT garage has written your name and the make, model and registration number of your vehicle in their appointments book, though; this will then cover you should you get pulled over by the police on your way there.

Now down to business: what should you be on the lookout for? First, bodywork. Generally, there should be no rot within 30cm of load-bearing metal or component mounting points. And if there's rust elsewhere, it must not pose a threat to anybody via jagged or sharp edges. This is particularly relevant to owners of elderly 4x4s

OPPOSITE Will your 4x4 easily pass the emissions part of the MoT test? If it's maintained well and serviced regularly – as with this Discovery V8 – it should have little difficulty *(Author)*

LEFT Checking your 4x4's lights before an MoT test is obvious but often overlooked. Don't forget brake lights, reversing lights and number-plate lights, too *(Author)*

BELOW If your 4x4 is fairly elderly, it's even more important that you carry out some obvious checks before taking it for its annual MoT test *(Frank Westworth)*

used primarily for off-road work, as this is the kind of usage that can have a major effect on bodywork condition and the pace of corrosion. With most such vehicles employing a sturdy separate chassis, you must also ensure that this crucial backbone of your 4x4 is in good order and not showing major signs of rot.

Before the MoT test, it pays to go over your 4x4's bodywork extremely carefully, on the lookout for any corrosion problems that may have started since last year. These are best dealt with now, before they become a major problem in the future. So even if that bit of rot near the sill isn't necessarily an MoT failure item this time round, it's cheaper and easier to deal with it now than when it poses a threat to roadworthiness later on, as I'm sure you'll agree.

Other areas that are easy to check prior to an MoT include lighting (don't forget your number plate lights, hazard warning lights and reversing

lights), wipers, windscreen washers and horn. Make sure all are working as they should. Also check that all seat belts (front and rear) are securely mounted and free of any fraying or other damage.

Now it's time to get your 4x4 on sturdy axle stands and get your hands dirty, firstly by checking out your vehicle's suspension. Assuming it's a fairly traditional, straightforward set-up, ensure the dampers are free of leaks and corrosion and that you inspect all areas – including springs – for potential damage. Also check out the condition of the wheel bearings by rocking the wheels, looking for excessive lateral movement. None of these basic tests at home will be as thorough as an MoT examiner's rigorous check-over, but they will at least give advance warning of major problem areas.

Moving on to the steering, check for excessive play in all the joints. As with the suspension, all rubber bushes should be examined, looking for splits and signs of perishing. Look for leaks from the steering box and make sure the latter is securely mounted.

It is also essential to give your brakes a thorough going over, from the levels and condition of your brake fluid (has it been changed in the last couple of years?) to the state of the shoes/pads, not forgetting to examine brake pipes and flexible hoses in the process. Also, make sure the parking brake is effective and properly adjusted.

Fluid level checks are vital before you venture out onto the road; we're talking clutch and brake fluid, engine oil (check it again the day after you change the oil), transmission and axle oils and, where applicable, damper fluid levels. Then there's the engine coolant: is the antifreeze mix strong enough (vital even in summer, as it helps reduce corrosion) and has the coolant been drained and replaced recently?

Don't forget to check your tyres. In the UK, each must have 1.6mm of tread depth across the central 75 per cent of the tread, around the whole tyre. Look for cracked sidewalls while you're at it – an increasingly common problem and a real pain, as it can mean an MoT failure even when there's ample tread remaining. Still, it's not worth messing about; not when you can receive three penalty points per tyre on your driving licence if you're caught driving with illegal rubber.

Then, of course, there's the emissions test, an area of concern primarily for owners whose vehicles are neglected, haven't been regularly serviced or have covered a massive mileage and are well past their best. If you care about your

4x4, having it serviced at the same time its MoT is due will probably reduce the chances of its failing the emissions section of the test.

As with other areas of this chapter, much of this MoT advice comes down to common sense, although it is often the smallest areas of preparation that get forgotten. So just because you've rebuilt the brakes and serviced the suspension on your 4x4, don't assume it'll sail through a test. Just a blocked washer jet or a split windscreen wiper rubber could put a stop to that. Don't let that happen to you. Be vigilant, and there's every chance of success.

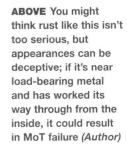

ABOVE You might think rust like this isn't too serious, but appearances can be deceptive; if it's near load-bearing metal and has worked its way through from the inside, it could result in MoT failure *(Author)*

LEFT Checking your tyres isn't just a question of measuring the tread depth; cracked sidewalls on older tyres will also result in MoT failure *(Author)*

Buying
a used 4x4

Making **sure**

Assuming you've already decided which secondhand 4x4 best suits your needs – and, just as importantly, which you can afford – it's time to get out and start checking out a few examples for sale. Before you do that, you need to know what you're looking for, what goes wrong and how you can best avoid getting ripped-off. And if you haven't actually decided on the make and model that tempts you most, don't worry: take a look at chapters seven to ten for essential advice on making the right choice.

Before we get on to the specifics of buying a secondhand 4x4, I'll just offer a few words of caution about buying used cars in general. At the best of times, it's a minefield of dangers and pitfalls; and when you see a 4x4 that seems to be exactly the one you've been searching high and low for, it's so easy to get carried away in the excitement and forget some basic procedures. That's when you're particularly vulnerable.

To begin with, when buying any used vehicle, only ever arrange to meet the vendor at their own home or (in the case of a dealer) at their premises. Meeting 'halfway' or arranging to have the car brought to your address is a classic ploy used by vendors who don't actually own the vehicles in question.

When you get to the vendor's house, ask to see (in the UK) the vehicle's V5C registration document and check that the vendor's name and the address shown on the V5C correspond with where you actually are. If you've any doubts or concerns, simply walk away. And if there's no V5C offered with the vehicle at all ('I haven't long moved house and the log book's still at DVLA', the vendor may claim), don't buy the vehicle under any circumstances, no matter how tempting it seems.

Checking the genuineness of a vehicle goes much further, though. Still with the V5C in your hand, take a look at the 4x4's VIN number; check it with the number that's printed on the V5C and, if there's any discrepancy whatsoever, don't even consider buying the car. It's that simple.

At this stage, and assuming you're examining a UK-spec 4x4 rather than a Japanese 'grey' import (which we'll deal with a little further on), you also need to be looking into the car's service history, to check that what the vendor claims to be a full service history actually is, as well as using this to help verify the mileage. Never accept a vendor's claim that '...the service book is still at the garage; I forgot to pick it up when I had the car serviced last week'. If a service history is boasted about, you want to be able to see it in front of you before you even consider making an offer.

Don't be afraid to spend time carefully studying the service book and any previous MoT certificates that are with the car, too. Check that all the mileages shown on certain dates seem to tally with what's being claimed about the vehicle. You might even want to make a note of the previous owner's name and address, approaching them before you hand over any money to ensure they can back up what you've been told and vouch for the car's history.

Another obvious point when viewing any used car is to look for signs of a forced entry, which relates to the previous point about checking out the vendor's actual ownership. It's a sad fact of life that many thousands of cars get broken into each year, so any signs of a previous break-in may simply have occurred during the current keeper's ownership; don't be afraid to ask, because there's no reason why they should hide this from you. If, however, you can clearly see that a door lock has been forced, the steering column shroud looks strangely loose or you can see

ABOVE Are you buying from a private source? If so, make sure you view it at the vendor's house rather than arranging to meet elsewhere. The address on the V5C should tally with where you actually are! (Richard Aucock)

OPPOSITE Can you be sure the mileage is genuine? Check out the 4x4's service history, MoTs and any old receipts for confirmation (Author)

LEFT Check all the details on the various identity plates with those shown on the V5C document. The VIN, in particular, should be absolutely identical (Author)

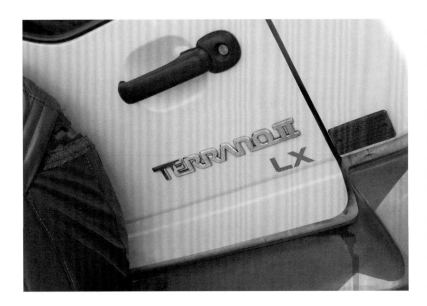

signs of shattered glass inside the 4x4, you've every right to have your suspicions aroused when the vendor denies all knowledge.

You also need to be on the lookout for signs of previous accident damage. Particularly on younger vehicles, check for mismatched paintwork (colour, finish and so on); ripples in body panels (possible evidence of body filler or poor repair work); signs of 'over-spray'; wheels that seem out of alignment; obvious replacement of 'inner' panel work under the bonnet. The list goes on, but just a couple of these points should be enough to make you suspicious and question the vendor's claim that '…she's never been in an accident'.

How thoroughly you follow this kind of advice will depend partly on how much you're paying for your secondhand 4x4, how old it is and what you're intending to use it for. Let's face it, checking for panel damage on a 15-year-old Lada Niva that's going to be used solely as a working tool is not going to be as important to you as it would be for the buyer of a 12-month-

ABOVE When looking for bodywork repairs, check the unevenness of any panel gaps and be on the lookout for differences in paint shades *(Author)*

BELOW Can you see any previous signs of a break-in? Check for forced locks and a damaged steering column shroud, for example. This Suzuki Grand Vitara seems genuine *(Author)*

old Range Rover. Be realistic in your approach, but always be on the lookout for vendors' stories that somehow just don't 'add up'.

One final point worth mentioning before we move on to a few specifics is this: professional car inspections, where you can pay for an expert to come along and thoroughly examine the vehicle you're thinking of buying. The AA and RAC carry out such inspections, as do many private companies and individuals. Obviously, if you paid next to nothing for a Suzuki with a fortnight's MoT left to run, it's not an economically viable proposition; on a vehicle of such value, you can't exactly expect perfection. But I'd advise anybody thinking of buying a more expensive used 4x4 to consider paying for an independent inspection. If they find any minor faults you might have missed, you'll be able to use this to negotiate the price downwards; and if they discover something major that makes you think twice about buying the car, surely that's also money well spent?

Such examinations usually include an HPI check (a vehicle-history checking service provided in the UK by HPI, the AA or the RAC) to ensure the 4x4 in question has never been registered as stolen, previously written-off in an accident or still has any outstanding finance against it. This is essential information, and it's available to anybody with a phone and a credit card to pay for it. Even if you decide against a full

independent inspection of a used vehicle, failure to have an HPI check carried out can be a very expensive lesson to learn. The difference in value between a 'clean' 4x4 and one that's been previously written-off and repaired can be 50 per cent or more, so we're talking serious money here. Before you buy any 4x4 of reasonable value, give HPI a call on 01722 422422 and get all the checks done. If everything is clear, surely that extra peace of mind is worth every penny of the cost?

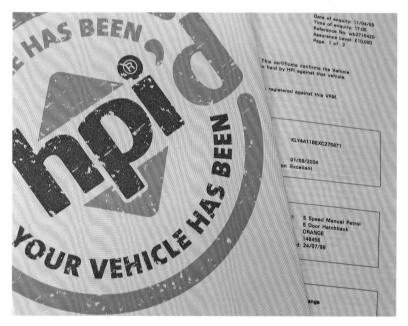

Import issues

Some – but by no means all – of what you've already read in this chapter won't necessarily apply if it's an unofficially imported 4x4 you're thinking of buying, one that's found its way over secondhand from Japan in recent years. The most popular 'grey' imports include the Mitsubishi Pajero, Toyota Surf, Mitsubishi Delica, Isuzu Bighorn and Mazda Bongo – though it's possible for just about any used 4x4 to end up in the UK as a used import from Japan. I even went to view a Land Rover Discovery V8 a while back that had recently been shipped over! And with over 30,000 secondhand cars arriving from Japan every year these days, there's plenty of 'grey' 4x4 choice available.

With any 'grey' import, you obviously need to carry out the same checks for accident damage, signs of abuse, VIN-number matching and so on; that's logical enough. But such issues as service history and previous MoTs aren't quite so straightforward.

One specialist importer of used Japanese-spec 4x4s I spoke to whilst writing this book was honest about the fact that he can't always guarantee the mileages of his vehicles. Having said that, 'clocking' (the winding back of a car's mileage) is far less of a problem in Japan than it is in the UK, which means that – as he's a decent trader with a good reputation – there's every chance that the vehicles on his forecourt

have never been tampered with in that way. However, not every used car dealer in the UK is as honest as him, and by the time a 'grey' 4x4 has found itself being bought and sold again a few times, there's no guarantee that its mileage is genuine. So, it seems, the onus is on the prospective purchaser to verify as much as possible.

The main problem is that a lot of Japanese imports don't come with a service history – and those that do are obviously written in Japanese, which makes deciphering them something of a challenge. Still, even a virtually unreadable service history is better than none, as it still might be possible to see roughly when servicing

OPPOSITE If you're lucky, your Japanese 'grey' import might just come with a full service history – but will you be able to understand any of it? *(Author)*

LEFT Many of the most popular 'grey' imports were also sold officially in the UK under different names, the Toyota Surf being known as the 4Runner... *(Author)*

...and the Isuzu Bighorn as the Trooper. Don't let daft names alone deter you from buying a 'grey' 4x4! *(Author)*

ABOVE Has your 'grey' 4x4 arrived only recently from Japan? If buying from a specialist importers, all duties and tests should have been dealt with and the vehicle correctly registered for UK use *(Author)*

BELOW Don't forget to look in the glovebox for any old receipts or previous MoTs if the vehicle was imported a while back. It might help to fill in any gaps in the service history *(Author)*

was carried out simply by studying some of the dates. But it's not always easy.

Similarly, if a used 4x4 has been in the UK only a matter of months, it clearly won't come with any previous MoT certificates to help verify its mileage – so you need to bear this in mind and be extra scrupulous when giving the vehicle the 'once over'.

So, when examining it throughout, not only are you looking for signs of neglect, abuse, accident damage and the like, you're also being vigilant about evidence of non-genuine mileage. If a mileage is indicated at 60,000, for example, you should be happy that the engine is reasonably rattle-free (though a lot of old turbo-diesel units can be clattery when cold, remember), that there's no excessive smoke when it is revved, the interior is tidy and not worn, the shock absorbers don't feel too soft or wallowing when cornering and the bodywork's general condition is in keeping with a vehicle of

LEFT Buy a well-maintained 'grey' import in tip-top condition, with all the legalities sorted out, and the process should be no more complicated than buying any other vehicle (Author)

such mileage. If you have any doubts at all, or the odd alarm bell is ringing in your head, it's time to look elsewhere – there's certainly no shortage of used 4x4 imports ('grey' or 'official') on sale.

In the UK, the best way of making sure you don't get stung when buying any 'grey' import is to make sure the supplying dealer is a member of the British Independent Motor Trade Association (BIMTA), an established organisation that, in the event of a dispute between a member of the public and an importer, can get involved and offer a conciliatory service – but only if the company concerned is a current member.

There's even more usefulness to BIMTA than that. When buying from a BIMTA member, make sure you ask them to provide an official BIMTA Certificate of Authenticity specifically for the 'grey' 4x4 you're interested in. Every year, BIMTA claims, around 2000 vehicles stolen in Japan end up being imported to the UK and sold on to unsuspecting buyers. But a BIMTA Certificate of Authenticity (which takes between five and ten working days to produce) will confirm whether or not a vehicle was ever registered as stolen prior to being exported from Japan, and will also prove there's no outstanding finance on it.

BIMTA can also provide odometer checks – and, again, this is a must if you're in any doubt about the imported 4x4 you're buying or the dealer you're buying it from. The vast majority of imports are sold in Japan via one of the country's 140 auction houses, and BIMTA has access to the records of almost all of them. This means an

official odometer check can ascertain how many kilometres a vehicle had covered by the time it went under the hammer in Japan, making it easy for any buyer to prove whether or not it has since been 'clocked'.

As long as the 'grey' 4x4 you're buying is registered in the UK, has passed an ESVA test (if applicable, as this only applies to vehicles under ten years of age), comes with a BIMTA Certificate of Authenticity and appears to be in decent condition, the risks involved are realistically no greater than when buying a UK-spec vehicle. But please, don't be tempted to cut corners in the hope of bagging a bargain.

BELOW Buying a 'grey'? Then obtaining a BIMTA certificate before you hand over any money is an excellent way of checking the genuineness of the 4x4 you're after (Author)

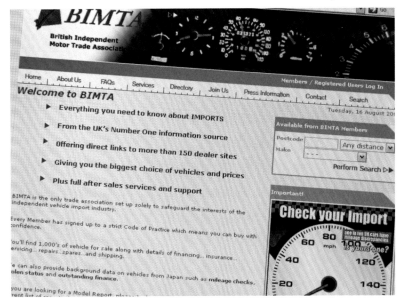

Fair wear and tear?

The issue of wear and tear is an awkward one when it comes to the world of 4x4s, for these vehicles are bought for such a vast range of tasks by all kinds of different owners. It's perfectly possible to come across an immaculate 4x4 of any make, model or age if it has been exceptionally well looked after. Equally, many of them are bought purely for hard work, and this will inevitably show in their condition on the used market.

The usage of 4x4s varies enormously. Yours might be nothing more than a daily user employed for the usual school run; on the other hand, it could be a hard-working farmer's tool, a towing vehicle for an extra-large caravan or a holdall for a rural-based builder. Whatever kind of use a vehicle has endured will have a major effect on its overall condition when you come to view.

As you'll read in chapter six, a very large proportion of 4x4s advertised for sale have been used for towing, whether that means a tiny camping trailer or a colossal caravan – and, as with any other vehicle, you need to be aware of the implications of this. Always try to find out what the vehicle regularly towed, and whether this falls well within its capabilities. If it's an example with manual transmission, does the clutch seem all right? Has the rear suspension been damaged by exceptionally heavy towing? Are the rear bumper and the bodywork around the towing bracket in perfect condition, or has the caravan/trailer had a few encounters with this while being hitched to the rear? Use plenty of common sense when viewing such a vehicle, and don't hesitate to say 'No thanks' if you're not happy with the overall condition.

Also remember that even if a 4x4 hasn't been bought simply to go mud-plugging, it can still suffer from off-road damage. Again, carry out all the usual checks that you would with any secondhand 4x4. Is there more mud and debris caked underneath than you'd expected? Are there any signs of dents and damage to the underside of the vehicle? Are the steering, brakes and various suspension components covered in thick mud, suggesting a lack of care? After even the mildest off-roading experience, any caring owner should thoroughly jet-wash the underside of their 4x4 to prevent serious build-up of mud. If it looks as if this hasn't taken place, I'd suggest you take a look at another 4x4 – unless, of course, this example seems spectacularly good value.

As I mentioned earlier, much of this comes down to common sense – and, inevitably, the rules do vary according to the age and price of the vehicle you're interested in purchasing. So if you're spending a modest amount on an MoT'd Suzuki Vitara, don't expect pristine bodywork, an immaculate interior and a shiny underside. On the other hand, if you're about to hand over a substantial sum for what's described as a Land Rover Discovery in tip-top condition, you've every right to expect such features. The market for secondhand 4x4s has never before offered so much choice; it's a case of finding the very best example for your budget.

OPPOSITE Look for obvious signs of damage caused by off-road terrain and mud. This kind of treatment can play havoc with alloy wheels, for example *(Author)*

LEFT After any kind of off-roading, your 4x4 should be thoroughly jet-washed. Encrusted mud can cause problems with the radiator, for instance, which can lead to overheating *(Author)*

BELOW One careful owner? It's important to ascertain the kind of use a 4x4 has had to endure, particularly if you're paying full retail price *(Author)*

What goes wrong?

Whatever kind of 4x4 you're thinking of buying, there are bound to be things that go wrong with it, either through age, mileage, or both. That's a simple fact of buying any used vehicle, even if it's a Japanese-built example with a world-beating reputation for reliability. No 4x4 is truly invincible – and you need to be prepared before you jump into any first-time purchase.

I've already discussed the petrol versus diesel argument in Chapter Two, so I won't waste space repeating myself here. Happily, in the case of most makes and models of 4x4, reliability levels are broadly the same whether it's a petrol or a diesel that temps you most.

Yet there are exceptions. Take the best-selling Land Rover Freelander, for example. It's not uncommon for 1.8-litre K-series petrol-engined versions to blow their head gaskets as the miles mount, whereas both the old L-series diesels and the later Td4 models tend not to suffer in the same way. That doesn't mean you shouldn't buy a secondhand Freelander with a K-series petrol engine; it essentially means you should be

It's particularly important to check thoroughly the suspension and steering of any secondhand 4x4 that you suspect may have been used off-road, as this can obviously accelerate the wear process. If the front ball joints are worn through heavy use or high mileage, these can be expensive to replace in some instances; look for signs of uneven tyre wear as an obvious clue. While we're on the subject of tyres, don't forget to remove the spare-wheel cover (assuming it's an externally-mounted spare wheel, of course) and check the tread and condition of the spare

aware of the issue and would be wise to buy the lowest-mileage example you can afford. It also makes it more important than ever to insist on a full service history.

When it comes to larger, family-size 4x4s such as Discoverys, Troopers, Shoguns, Terranos and the like, diesel sales have always heavily exceeded those of the petrol-engined versions, primarily because of the former's far superior fuel economy. There's every chance you'll find a turbo-diesel 4x4 of such size ideal for your needs, but you'll need to be prepared to pay for the privilege. A turbo-diesel Discovery holds its value better than a petrol-engined V8 version, and it's the same with the oil-burning Troopers, Terranos, Shoguns and Pajeros and their V6 petrol equivalents. The depreciation curve is far steeper with a thirsty petrol-powered 4x4 because of the extra daily running costs.

Most diesel 4x4s, despite having the added complication of a turbocharger, are pretty robust machines, although it's worth ensuring the turbo unit itself is fully functioning before you hand over your cash. Excessive smoke from a diesel's exhaust can be a sign of turbo wear – or, if you're lucky, simply a case of worn injectors. You'll also need to check that, as the revs rise in each gear, you can feel the turbo spinning into action; it won't be in the same kind of neck-snapping way that you'd expect from a turbocharged performance car, but you should still feel a subtle increase in acceleration as the turbo starts to do its job. If you've any doubts, it may be worth getting an independent inspection carried out before you buy; and if the vendor claims there's been a new turbo fitted in the last year or two, insist on seeing a receipt or guarantee to prove this.

Most standard 4x4 transmissions are generally reliable, though you need to ensure the synchromesh isn't prematurely worn through abuse or over-work. Many automatic gearboxes can be a little sluggish to change gear when cold, but this isn't necessarily a sign of wear.

RIGHT Hard-workers, such as the Daihatsu Fourtrak, are often abused and neglected by previous owners. Fortunately, most are mechanically strong enough to cope *(Author)*

BELOW A turbo-diesel-powered Discovery holds its value better than any V8 petrol-engined version, such is the difference in fuel economy between the two *(Author)*

itself – easily overlooked in your determination to be vigilant.

Modern power-assisted steering systems tend to be reliable even at high mileages, though it's not unusual to see leaks from the power-steering box in some instances. While you're under there, check for engine and transmission oil leaks, too – not necessarily a major problem, depending on your expectations, but certainly something you should be aware of.

Assuming the 4x4's braking system is fairly standard in design, there should be few things to worry about on a well-maintained vehicle, though it's not unknown to come across examples with warped front discs. Check this whilst you're taking a look at the whole braking circuit for signs of neglect and wear.

LEFT Checking over the suspension of any well-used 4x4 you're thinking of buying is essential. Look for obvious leaks, signs of wear, split rubbers and so on *(Author)*

BELOW Buying a 4x4 with a dual-range transfer box? Make sure it works in all settings and it switches from two- to four-wheel drive (and back again) with ease *(Author)*

Another major mechanical concern, of course, is the state of the vehicle's dual-range transfer box, so you must ensure it's functioning as it should. Most used 4x4s offer rear-wheel drive for standard road use, with four-wheel drive being easily selected via either a lever by the gearstick or a dashboard-mounted button. You then have a choice of high- or low-ratio all-wheel drive, depending on the severity of the off-road situation or the levels of grip and low-down torque you require. Some 4x4s (Land Rovers and Range Rovers included) offer full-time four-wheel drive, with high ratio employed for road use and low ratio easily selected for tough terrain.

Whichever system the 4x4 you're thinking of buying comes with, you need to make sure it's working well and isn't showing signs of wear. In the case of a part-time system with a standard

dual-range transfer box, for example, make sure you can select four-wheel drive in both high and low ratios, and then back again to rear-wheel drive without difficulty. Does the relevant '4x4' warning light show up on the dashboard? Do the transfer box changes happen almost instantly, as well as first time, every time? You should always try any such 4x4 in all three different drive modes before you agree to buy it, just to ensure it's doing what it was intended to do.

The transfer box itself is usually a robust, reliable and trustworthy piece of engineering, as well as surprisingly simple in principle. But years of hard off-road work or a lifetime of regular abuse (perhaps with four-wheel drive being selected at highly inappropriate speeds) can have a long-term negative effect. You can't be too careful.

LEFT While checking the tyres all round, don't forget the spare! It's probably hiding under a protective cover and could be illegally worn without your even noticing *(Author)*

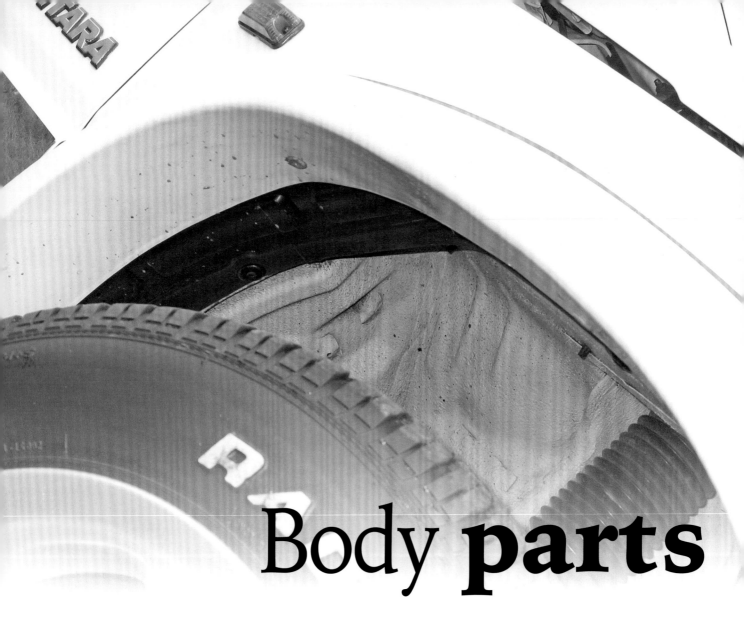

Body parts

An important part of buying any used 4x4 is to pay careful attention to its bodywork and underside, although your priorities will vary according to the age and price of the vehicle in question. As I pointed out earlier, it's unfair to expect a cheap and cheerful decade-old 4x4 to be in cosmetically pristine condition – but if it comes with a current MoT and is claimed to be in good condition, then it should at least be structurally sound and capable of regular, safe use.

No matter how tough or reliable a 4x4 may be by reputation, it's important to remember that any neglected, hard-working vehicle will eventually rust. It's a fact of life. Even an older Land Rover with the majority of its body panels made from aluminium still uses a steel chassis, steel foot wells and steel inner sections – and that can mean MoT-failing corrosion in many cases.

It's no different for the plethora of ageing Japanese 4x4s, whose reputation for mechanical reliability and longevity is simply unrivalled but whose propensity to rust is well known. It's by no means rare to see elderly Isuzu Troopers, Daihatsu Fourtraks, Mitsubishi Shoguns and Toyota Land Cruisers with their steel panels eaten away by rot, despite the fact that their mechanical parts are still in tip-top working order.

Before you start inspecting any used 4x4's bodywork and chassis, don't forget to get clear in your mind what's really important to you. If you don't mind the odd bit of superficial corrosion on a wheel arch or along the bottom of a door because you're a realist and you know you're not paying a lot for the vehicle anyway, that's fine – assuming the vehicle is still structurally sound, of course. But if you're paying more and you expect your used 4x4 to be impressively smart too, then read on.

Every 4x4 has its own particular weak areas when it comes to bodywork and corrosion, though the same basic rules apply in most cases. Pay particular attention, for example, to front wings (particularly around light units and the extremities of the wheel arches), the rear arches, the tailgate, the bottoms of all doors and the sills. Beware of any plastic wheel-arch extensions that are fitted, as these can hide serious rust chomping away behind them. Don't assume that a bit of bubbling paintwork is just that; it's invariably a sign of something far more sinister, and will be the result of rust working its way from the inside outwards.

Rust can also break out around the windscreen, a difficult job to have repaired properly on any vehicle. In any case, if the 4x4 you're looking at is so rusty round its screen that it needs welding repairs, you have to ask yourself whether the inevitably dubious state of the rest of the vehicle makes the task worthwhile.

It's not unusual to find a rotten floor on an elderly 4x4, even if the vehicle sits on a sturdy separate chassis that in most cases is fairly resilient. Years of serious off-roading can take their toll if the previous owner hasn't bothered to clean the underside on a regular basis. There are plenty of mud traps under most 4x4s to start encouraging the rusting process.

The good news about many of the scruffier used 4x4s you may come across is that, despite appearances, they can still be structurally sound. No 4x4 is going to fail its MoT because of surface rust, paint chips, grazes and scrapes – so if you're not too fussy about cosmetics, you might be able to pick up a bargain. Don't confuse cosmetic tattiness with MoT-failing structural corrosion, though.

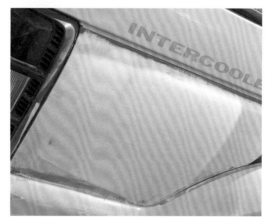

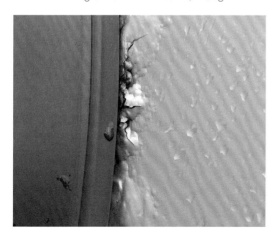

LEFT How bothered are you about the cosmetics of a secondhand 4x4? It will probably depend on the age of the vehicle and its asking price *(Author)*

LEFT Not all evidence of poorly repaired previous accident damage will be this obvious! It pays to be vigilant and to take your time *(Author)*

LEFT It may look unsightly, but the rust on this Suzuki SJ is still easily repairable at this stage. Catch it early enough and it makes for far easier treatment *(Author)*

FAR LEFT This may not look too serious, but behind the plastic wheel-arch extension sits major rot that's eating away at what's left of this Shogun's front wing *(Author)*

LEFT The lower rear quarter of this Shogun is showing obvious signs of inside-to-out corrosion and will need major repair work *(Author)*

Where to find them

Narrowing down your choice of secondhand 4x4 isn't the only major decision to be made here. You also need to consider whether you'll be buying privately, from a trader or even at a car auction.

Buying your used 4x4 from a dealer certainly brings the greatest consumer rights, with more comeback available to you if things go wrong. Buying from a dealer in the UK means you're covered by the Sale of Goods Act, which essentially means that the 4x4 on which you're spending your hard-earned cash must meet an acceptable standard. It's also a relatively simple way of buying, as you can peruse several vehicles on one dealer's forecourt without the need to travel great distances viewing ones that have been advertised privately.

As ever, there are pitfalls to be aware of. First of all, you need to ensure the dealer you're talking to is a member of a trade association, such as the Retail Motor Industry Federation in the UK – or, if it is a company specialising in 'grey' imports, BIMTA (mentioned earlier in the chapter). Secondly, you need to ensure you understand exactly the terms under which the vehicle is being sold to you.

For example, is the dealer claiming some kind of warranty is included in the sale – and, if so, has he given you an opportunity to study the small print, the various exclusions and, of course, confirm the timescale of the warranty? Some dealers offer their own 30-day all-inclusive warranty, while others will try to sell you a one- two- or even three-year independent used-car warranty – on which they will obviously be earning commission. Use a warranty as a useful haggling tool, but make sure you understand exactly what is and isn't part of its coverage.

You also need to be realistic about the age of the 4x4 you're buying from a dealer, as your consumer rights are, in essence, affected by this. You have every legal right to expect a twelve-month-old 4x4 purchased from a dealer to be in superb condition throughout, unless he states otherwise. But a ten- or fifteen-year-old example

will inevitably have experienced wear and tear – which means that if the exhaust fails, the brake pads need replacing or the battery dies after a few days of ownership, you'll have very little cause for complaint. It's an old vehicle and, quite simply, parts do wear out. It's a fact of life.

Before buying any used 4x4 from a dealer, you should also check the terms of the sale itself, as elderly vehicles are often marked on invoices as 'trade sales'. This is even firmer proof that you're

OPPOSITE Are you thinking of buying your secondhand 4x4 from a car dealer? In theory, it should mean you're covered by the Sale of Goods Act *(Author)*

LEFT It pays to read the small print of any used-car warranty very carefully. Official manufacturers' used-car schemes are often considered the best, even if you sometimes pay slightly more for the vehicles as a result *(Author)*

BELOW If you're buying your secondhand 4x4 from a private source, the only legal requirement for the vendor is that it must be 'as described' *(Author)*

N443 YRM

RIGHT At any auction, read the information sheets on the windscreens very carefully; they'll tell you what you need to know about mileage, MoT and much more (Author)

165F

Direct from

Main Agent

R447AKL
Date 1st Registered in UK: 14/01/1998

**Land Rover Discovery Turbo Diesel
TDi Hard Top 3dr**

Mileage:
UNWARRANTED

Vat Status:
PLUS VAT

Documents:
V5/2 here
Tax: None
MoT: Nov '04
Service History

Mechanical Description:

**NO MAJOR
MECHANICAL FAULTS**

Easters Court, Leominster, Herefordshire, HR6 0DE.
Tel: 01568 611325 Fax: 01568 614454 www.brightwells.com

Brightwells

The Auctioneers have received the details shown here but cannot
guarantee that this lot is correctly described herein.

All vehicles are sold on the Auctioneer's description only.

BELOW It pays to get to the auction early to do your viewing. Once a vehicle is in the auction ring, you don't get long to make your mind up (Author)

buying the vehicle 'as seen', you're happy to take the risk and there are no guarantees as to its condition. It can be a good way of grabbing a bargain, but not if you're a cautious buyer who doesn't enjoy taking the odd risk.

Buying privately can also be a risky business, although it can save you money. The only real legal obligation of a private seller is that the vehicle must be sold 'as described' – and that's about it. The seller isn't obliged to offer any kind of guarantees, you won't get a warranty and it's unlikely you'll be able to part-exchange your old car. On the other hand, a private seller doesn't have the overheads of a trader, which means you can often get a used 4x4 cheaper this way.

The most effective way of taking the risk out of buying privately is to ensure you get an HPI check carried out, as detailed earlier on in this chapter. And, as already mentioned, it's worth considering a professional car inspection by an independent expert. It could save you a considerable sum in the long run.

LEFT It's amazing just what a varied selection of used 4x4s comes up for auction every week at the Brightwells specialist sale; it's well worth a visit *(Author)*

The third major source of used 4x4s, of course, is an auction house, although most general car auctions feature only a small percentage of 4x4s among their more mainstream stock. The solution to this in the UK is to travel to Leominster in Herefordshire on a Tuesday morning, to Brightwells auctioneers (see www.brightwells.com for details) and their weekly specialist 4x4 sale. Upwards of 250 4x4s of all makes, models and ages pass through the Brightwells sale every week, so there's sure to be something suitable for most budgets. Log on to the company website for details of forthcoming entries and further information.

Car auctions in general bring their own set of rules and consumer rights, of which you should be aware before you attend. For a start, there's usually no opportunity to test drive any vehicles being sold at auction, as the sales process happens so quickly. Also, those auction houses offering any 4x4s with what they call a 'trial' will be giving some kind of guarantee on the condition of the engine and transmission only – with absolutely nothing else included. Most older vehicles are 'sold as seen', which means no comeback whatsoever. Bear in mind, too, that an auction house will charge a buyer's premium on top of what your winning bid is, so you need to find out how much this is before you bid. And, of course, don't forget that your winning bid is legally binding and means you have entered into a contract with the auctioneers from which you are then unable to withdraw.

What many people don't realise is that similar rules and regulations apply to internet auction sites as they do to traditional auction houses, so don't be tempted to enter a bid on a vehicle listed on eBay 'as a bit of a laugh' unless you're serious about buying it. If you win the online auction and don't proceed with the purchase for any reason, the vendor has every right to take legal proceedings against you.

So are auctions a good idea? Well, they can certainly yield some bargains. But they're not for the fainthearted, and buyers should take every precaution before placing a bid. Get it right, though (ideally, taking somebody along with you to help check over the vehicles you're interested in), and you can end up with a trade-price 4x4 that's exactly what you've been looking for. It does happen.

LEFT Thinking of buying from an internet auction site? Don't forget that the same basic rules apply – including the obligations of any winning bidder *(Author)*

Venturing
off-road

What's it capable of?

You've finally taken the plunge and bought yourself a 4x4, probably one that you're going to press into immediate everyday service. You'll doubtless find it ideal for your on-road needs and will be delighted with your choice. But, as you've suspected all along, there's far more to owning a 4x4 than driving it on tarmac. Or rather, there should be.

It's become a bit of a cliché in recent years that the nearest most 4x4s get to going off-road is mounting the kerb outside Sainsbury's, and in many cases it's actually (and rather sadly) true. Many of the 'school run specials' suffer no tougher an existence than the average family saloon, despite so many 4x4s being designed and engineered to enjoy life in the rough. So why not break with suburban tradition and really get to know your 4x4 where it truly belongs, away from the black stuff?

Before you head for the hills (or woods, farmland, or disused quarry…), you need to get an idea of what your particular make and model of 4x4 is capable of in the rough. The last thing you want to do is inflict some kind of major damage on it, which will end up costing you serious money to put right. So the first piece of advice has to be: keep your aspirations realistic.

If, for example, you own a compact family-style soft-roader that was designed more for the tarmac than the mountainside (Hyundai Santa Fe, Honda HR-V, Toyota RAV4 and Kia Sportage spring to mind), don't expect to be able to tackle the kind of serious off-road terrain normally reserved for the Land Rover Defenders of this world. It's not that your road-inspired 4x4 isn't capable of going off-road (for plainly it is, thanks to its all-wheel drive and, in most cases, its dual-range transfer box); it's just that its suspension will have been developed with on-road handling and ride quality primarily in mind, its tyres will be standard road-going items and its monocoque-style bodyshell won't be as rigid as that of the Land Rover with the traditional separate chassis. Then, of course, its lack of such useful off-road features as a locking differential may limit severe rough-stuff progress, while its relatively high-revving petrol powerplant (in many cases) will be all but useless when it comes to seriously effective downhill engine braking.

What I'm saying, therefore, is by all means head off-road in just about any 4x4 you happen to own or are thinking of buying – but don't push the vehicle beyond its capabilities. This means choosing the kind of away-from-the-tarmac terrain

that suits the 4x4 you're driving, and if that results in your being limited to semi-rough tracks or some of the easier green lanes that are dotted around the UK (more details of which further on), then so be it.

Don't assume that most affordable 4x4s were originally built solely for on-road use. The large numbers of enthusiasts now using easily-modified Suzuki Vitaras, SJs and Samurais primarily off-road – often to huge effect, much to the embarrassment of some Land Rover owners – is proof of this. They have a basic but effective mechanical layout, two-range transfer box, separate chassis and enough ground clearance to enable them to be taken to amazing lengths. But we'll cover this in more detail further on in the book.

OPPOSITE Not using over-aggressive tyres when green laning may sound like obvious advice, but it's important such rights of way aren't abused *(Land Rover)*

LEFT Even the family holdall you use for towing the caravan can make a great rough-stuff plaything, perfect for the occasional weekend off-roader *(Author)*

BELOW The Suzuki SJ's basic mechanical layout, separate chassis, simple design and light weight all contribute to its surprising off-road capabilities *(Author)*

Driving off-road

Driving off-road isn't simply a case of steering away from a boring stretch of tarmac and into the nearest mud. Far from it. It involves preparation, planning, common sense and a few strict rules that should never be broken if you and your vehicle are to remain safe and unharmed.

It goes without saying that you should know and understand the basic operation of your vehicle, where all of the major controls are situated and how to operate the lights, windscreen wipers and so on. That may seem like pretty standard stuff, but it's always a good idea to remind yourself of the location of all such controls.

You should also know where the spare wheel and jack are located and where all of the jacking and towing points can be found. Before venturing off-road, ensure that the vehicle is in fine working order and make sure you check all fluid and oil levels and, of course, tyre pressures.

It is vital to know and understand the strengths and weaknesses of your 4x4, as this is the only way of finding its true potential. Be certain that you know how to engage low-range four-wheel drive, how the all-wheel-drive system operates and how to work the freewheeling front hubs (if fitted).

You should also know and understand the type of tyres fitted to your vehicle. Most new 4x4s come with either standard road-going rubber or, if you're lucky, what's known as 'all-terrain' tyres. Both of these are great for road use, and the latter can also tackle reasonable off-road situations – but they do have their limitations. This means that extremely muddy areas should be avoided as you'll almost certainly get stuck at some point. The obvious solution to this, of course, is to invest in some proper off-road tyres for your 4x4, a subject we'll be covering in more detail in Chapter Eleven.

Other areas to consider are your 4x4's ground clearance (the amount of space beneath its lowest point), as well as approach, departure and ramp break-over angles. These refer to (in order) the steepness of a slope you can drive up to without catching the front bumper; the steepness of a slope you can drive from without catching the rear bumper; and the angle of a crest that can be taken without grounding the vehicle in the middle. These are critical factors for serious off-road enthusiasts, with poor approach and departure angles, in particular, seriously limiting the kind of inclines and off-road challenges you can enjoy. Generally, the shorter your vehicle's wheelbase and the smaller the front and rear overhangs, the better it is for off-roading – but it's still a good idea to talk to other off-roaders about their own experiences.

When driving off-road in tricky terrain, always engage low-ratio four-wheel drive before tackling any ground that looks remotely soft or rough. The control it gives is immense and, if ground conditions change suddenly, you will have time to react. And always travel slowly off road; speed, except in very specific circumstances, is unnecessary, uncomfortable and can do untold damage to your vehicle.

Before you even get that far, a crucial piece of driving advice is always to keep your thumbs on the outside of the steering wheel when driving off-road; this means that if the wheel is suddenly 'tugged' while you are crossing particularly rough

ABOVE If the driver of this Series II Discovery had invested in a set of off-road tyres, he might have avoided getting stuck so dramatically! *(Author)*

OPPOSITE Keeping your thumbs on the outside of the steering wheel is essential when off-roading; otherwise it's all too easy for the wheel to 'snatch' and for injury to occur *(Isuzu)*

LEFT Safe and responsible off-roading demands a degree of forward planning. It's not just a case of jumping in and heading for the mud *(Author)*

RIGHT Short-wheelbase Land Rovers are a perennial favourite among hardened off-roaders, thanks to good ground clearance and an impressive lack of front and rear overhang *(Author)*

BELOW What the Suzuki SJ lacks in low-down torque and engine braking, it makes up for in sheer get-up-and-go *(Author)*

terrain, your thumbs won't get broken in the process. Be ready to grip the wheel firmly should the need arise, but don't fight with it as you head off-road; smooth, steady progress is the order of the day. And before you even think about tackling any off-road course, make sure (kitted out in suitable clothing and boots, of course) that you literally walk it first; there's no finer way of getting to know its pitfalls and its biggest challenges than by covering it on foot.

When tackling a moderately rough track or a dry field in a 4x4, you will probably find high-ratio all-wheel drive more than adequate for your needs. For anything more severe, you will need to select the low-ratio setting on your transfer box, as this will enable you to make slow,

low-geared progress over some surprisingly challenging terrain.

Which gear you choose to pull away in – and sometimes even continue to drive in – when off-roading will depend on the type of 4x4 you're piloting. Fairly high-revving petrol-engined off-roaders (a Suzuki Vitara, for example) will be most suited to first-gear start-offs. But if you're lucky enough to have a lower-revving diesel-engined off-roader at your disposal, with its extra low-down torque, then pulling away (and maintaining progress) in second gear is ideal. Meanwhile, low-range third or fourth gears can be good for traversing sand, mud, off-road snow and certain tricky tracks once you're under way.

The advantages of a lower-revving, higher-torque diesel engine in a 4x4 can be significant, for it means a more effortless and confidence-inspiring experience. Pulling away in second gear over particularly tricky terrain makes sense, but

RIGHT The ramp break-over angle of your 4x4 is important in this situation; too long a wheelbase or too low a ground clearance and you could have problems *(Author)*

once under way you can then remove your feet from the accelerator and brake pedals and let the low engine revs do all the work for you. All that diesel-engine torque will see your 4x4 making steady progress when driven this way; and when you come to a diffcult downhill slope, you'll find the low-down torque providing impressive engine braking, so you won't need to touch the brake pedal and risk skidding, as the low gearing and torque combination itself will keep the machine moving at a slow and predictable rate.

Engine braking in a petrol-powered 4x4 is generally poorer and should be relied upon less. It's important, therefore, to ensure you don't get yourself into any potentially dangerous situations that are beyond the capabilities of your vehicle. The safety of you and your passengers is paramount, and it is necessary to remember that not every 4x4 is capable of tackling every off-road situation.

Remember, too, that it's important to learn from others' mistakes (previous vehicle tracks might indicate trouble spots, for example), that you drive at a sensible speed at all times (off-roading is about steady progress above all else), and that you act responsibly by never crossing steep slopes laterally – or you might find your vehicle tipping over with alarming ease.

Making sure your vehicle is fully prepared, your mind is focused, your driving style is smooth and steady and your common sense is working overtime, you should be able to enjoy some very effective off-road action with minimal drama. But, you know, there's really no substitute for getting some professional, practical advice – and there's more of this readily available now than ever before.

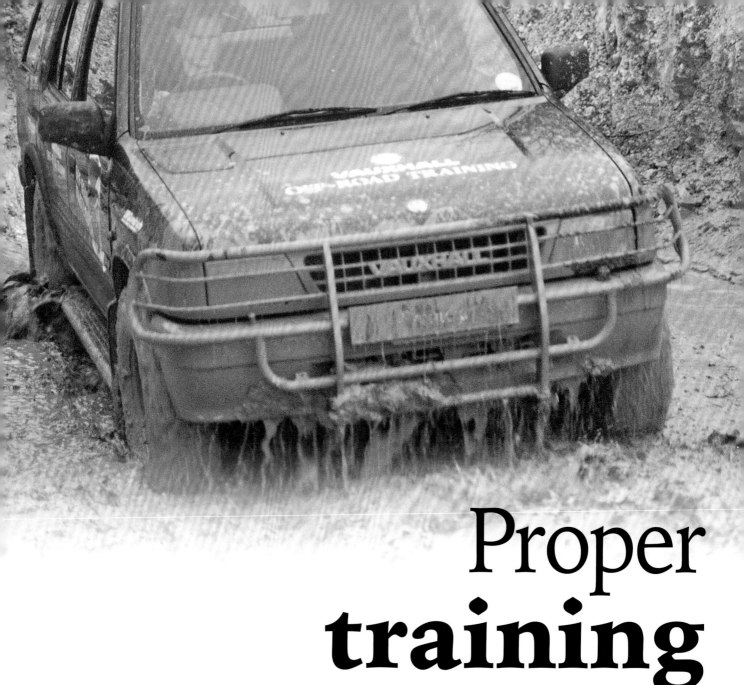

Proper training

Assuming you're a first-time off-road driver, I'd thoroughly recommend some kind of proper training before you actually head for the rough stuff – and this is something that is both easily arranged and competitively priced. You see, no matter how much detail I went into in the pages of this book, it would be no substitute for actually getting out there and experiencing it all for yourself with an expert by your side.

Decent training can be hugely beneficial to both you and your 4x4, as it means you'll learn the safest of off-road driving styles, as well as being taught how to get the most from your vehicle without damaging it or shortening its lifespan. You can also learn about such techniques as winching and self-recovery, essential if you're about to embark upon off-roading as a serious hobby and you want to get the most from modifying your vehicle. Whatever your level of interest – from casual curiosity to full-scale obsession – I can't over-emphasise the benefit of sound training.

So where do you go for this? In the UK, a good first step is to contact the British Off-Road Driving Association (BORDA), an organisation founded in 1996 to ensure high standards among off-road driver-training operators. Its members all adhere to a strict set of rules and guidelines, and offer various levels of driver training depending upon the trainee's own needs and aspirations. Take a look at the BORDA website (www.borda.org.uk) to find your nearest operating member and to discuss which course would suit you best.

You may also be interested in joining an off-road club and using the experience of its members to guide you on your way. This can be an excellent idea, as it can also open up a whole new social life for you – particularly on all those damp wintry afternoons you hitherto hated! Take a look at any of the general all-wheel-drive magazines (such as *4x4 Mart* and *4x4*) or dedicated Land Rover publications (including *Land Rover World* and *Land Rover Monthly*) for up to date lists of both national and regional 4x4 clubs. It's a great way of learning about your vehicle, what it's capable of and how you can really get into the off-road scene.

OPPOSITE If you're serious about having fun off-road in a safe and responsible manner, there's no substitute for decent professional training *(Vauxhall)*

LEFT For safety in these conditions, proper training will be time well spent *(Author)*

BELOW Another way of enjoying your off-road experience in a controlled environment is to join a club and take part in its various activities *(Author)*

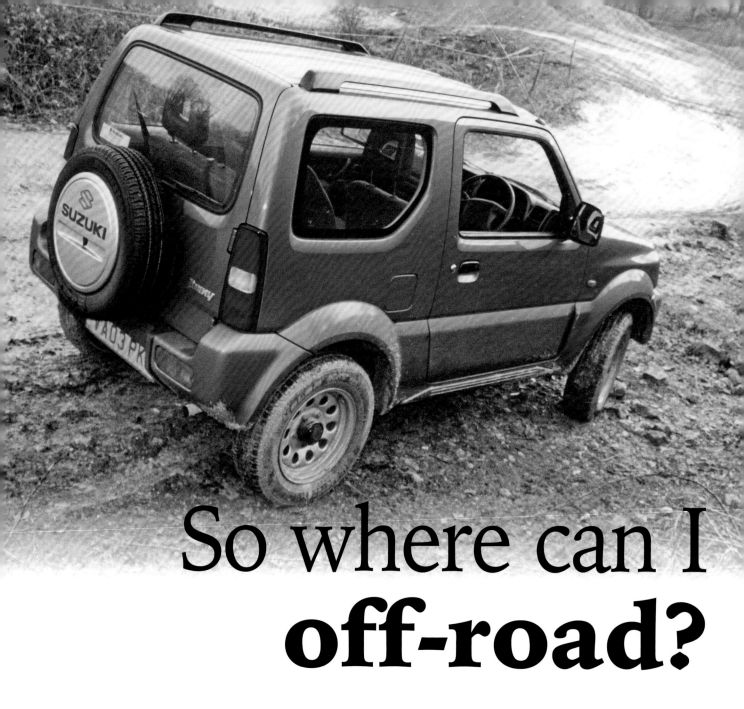

So where can I off-road?

Public attitudes towards off-road drivers have varied over the years, with some members of the green lobby blaming 4x4 owners for desecration of the countryside. It's true that a minority of 4x4 owners have spoiled it for others in the past by driving off-road where they strictly shouldn't, and no doubt there has been both damage caused and tempers frayed as a result. But to suggest that anybody who drives off-road is acting irresponsibly is plain nonsense.

Nevertheless, anybody embarking upon off-road driving for the first time has a duty to bear in mind the needs of other users of the countryside, and it is absolutely essential for the future of off-road activities that vehicles are taken only where they are legally allowed to be.

Happily, this isn't too difficult these days, thanks to the number of companies and organisations offering off-road courses and rural venues for 4x4 owners. Yes, it costs the driver to take part, as you'll find a little further on when we deal with the topic of off-road fun days. But surely it's better to pay a relatively small fee for the privilege of having fun, content in the knowledge nobody else can come along and spoil your enjoyment?

A vital part of the off-road scene is Britain's plethora of green lanes, better described as unsurfaced rights of way, which can be found throughout the country. At the time of writing, many of them allow suitable vehicles to legally access them, as long as they're four-wheel drives or off-road motorcycles specifically designed for rough-stuff usage. Just because rights of way are unsurfaced, doesn't mean they're immune from the rules of the road, hence any vehicle travelling along a green lane should still be taxed, MoT'd and insured as normal.

Locating green lanes in your area is a case of looking at the very latest Ordnance Survey Landranger map for the region and, ideally, checking for rights of way on the definitive map held by your local authority. Every local council should have a Rights of Way Officer to help you with this and to confirm where exactly you are allowed to drive.

Finding a suitable green lane is just the start of it, for there are certain unofficial 'rules' that ought to be adhered to if we are to retain our rights of way for future use. For example, it's recommended that you never drive faster than 10–12mph along any green lane, which will aid the safety of both you and other users of the right of way – walkers and cyclists included. Make sure you respect the rights of others to be there and show them some consideration as a result; it will go some way towards convincing anti-4x4 campaigners that we can be a considerate lot.

It's also recommended you don't use over-aggressive tyres when green laning. If a green lane is so muddy or inaccessible that it requires the ultimate in off-road rubber, should you really be there churning up what remains of it? On the other hand, don't attempt a green lane with standard road-going tyres as you're likely to get stuck at the first sign of mud.

Another invaluable piece of advice is never to tackle a green lane alone. Ideally, always have at least one other vehicle with you, capable of towing you out of any trouble. And make sure every vehicle taking part is fitted with secure tow points and is equipped with such essential equipment as a strong recovery rope (not a standard tow rope).

If you're tempted by the idea of taking your 4x4 along a selection of green lanes, be warned: these rights of way may not always be there for us to use. At the time of writing, pressure is increasing to change the law and restrict the use of motorised vehicles along what have previously been public rights of way. There's every chance

such access will be taken away from 4x4 enthusiasts in the future. By treating green lanes and their many different users with respect in the meantime, we may be able to go some way towards convincing 'the powers that be' that such legislation would be unfair. Time will tell.

To find out more about green lanes, you should contact the Green Lane Association (via www.glass-uk.org) and talk to them about rights of way in your area, find out about any organised green-lane activities and gain useful advice on how to go about green laning for the very first time. Some of these ancient rights of way make for fascinating experiences – but it's essential they're treated with respect.

Joining an off-road club will, of course, open up all sorts of new off-roading opportunities for you, with organised club events at specific locations enabling you to really make the most of your 4x4's capabilities in a controlled environment. But what if you don't necessarily want to belong to a club, but you like the idea of informal off-roading as and when you can find the time? Well, there is an alternative.

OPPOSITE Ensuring 4x4s are driven off-road only where they're legally allowed to be is essential for maintaining rights of way and respecting the needs of other users of the countryside *(Author)*

BELOW Further information on green lanes can be obtained from the Green Lane Association; check out its website for full details *(Author)*

Off-road
fun days

The rise in popularity of 4x4s has seen a corresponding increase in the number of off-road fun days being organised throughout the UK. In essence, these are strictly non-competitive events organised by specialist companies or individuals, often hosted in disused quarries or on rural farmland, where owners of 4x4s can turn up, pay a fee and go and have lots of fun playing in the mud. Simple, you'd think.

Well, yes. But there have been some negative comments about off-road fun days in recent years, sometimes from 4x4 clubs who organise their own events specifically for members. Such clubs tend to put great emphasis on driver training and safety – areas they have accused other events organisers of ignoring. But is this actually so?

To find out, I spoke with Richard Walsh of 4x4 Funday Ltd, who insisted that safety and the right kind of advice are both paramount at his events. For a start, spectators are not allowed at Richard's events, which means there's no chance of onlookers being injured and, of course, there are fewer distractions for the drivers. Secondly, if a total novice turns up at a fun day unsure of just how to drive off-road, Richard and his colleagues are on hand to offer guidance, advice and safety tips to make sure the 4x4 owner gets the most out of it.

Do all drivers take notice of this? In theory, anybody can take a 4x4 to a fun day, thrash it to within an inch of its life and end up inflicting serious damage upon it by ignoring the advice of the experts. But how many owners will really entertain this idea with their own 4x4s? I've yet to see any.

There's a risk involved in any activity which involves vehicles. But surely it all comes down to minimising that risk and simply ensuring that driving standards are maintained. Remember, too, that off-road fun days are strictly non-competitive – and that means most drivers have a cool head and are surprisingly courteous and patient when it comes to others taking part.

Obviously, if events organisers are unhappy with the antics of any of their entrants, they reserve the right to ask them to leave. In reality, this step very rarely needs to be taken. In my experience, most enthusiasts are there simply to enjoy themselves responsibly and to see just what their vehicles are capable of.

One final word of advice: although you'll be asked to sign a disclaimer when you take part in any fun day, essentially making yourself responsible for any damage to your vehicle or anything that is obviously your own fault, you should ensure the organiser has public liability insurance. Don't be afraid to ask to see a copy of the insurance certificate if you're unsure.

OPPOSITE AND ABOVE For fun in the mud that's legal and organised, you might want to consider an off-road fun day; increasing numbers of 4x4 owners now regularly take part *(Author)*

LEFT Off-road fun days are strictly non-competitive, which obviously helps reduce the risk of accidents and vehicle damage *(Author)*

Giving it a go

During the time I was writing this book, I found myself at Much Wenlock in Shropshire, England on a cold, wintry morning. It was all thanks to an invitation from 4x4 Funday Ltd, a small organisation that – as mentioned already – specialises in organising off-road days that enable 4x4 owners to really enjoy themselves while testing the capabilities of their vehicles.

Richard Walsh has had exclusive rights to the use of Farley Quarry at Much Wenlock for some time, but this was my first opportunity to get along and experience it for myself. At the time of writing, events are held here at least once a month throughout the year – and with anything between 30 and 50 vehicles turning up on a typical day, it can be quite a spectacle.

Spectacle it may be, but that doesn't mean spectators are allowed. In fact, they're very much a no-no, for obvious safety reasons. You can, though, bring along friends and family within your vehicle, with up to two drivers allowed for a single payment.

Yes, it may be cheaper to join an off-road club and take part in their organised events instead; but with a more informal fun day, you have much more freedom to take part in exactly what you want to, when you want to. You can spend a whole day having a pretty exciting time out in the quarry, if you so wish, and if there are two drivers taking part in one vehicle, they can share the costs. Not bad for a few hours of fun and learning, surely?

One of the most fascinating ways in which fun days have changed over the years is in the sheer variety of 4x4s they're now attracting. The event we took part in at Farley Quarry was proof of that. You can bring any 4x4 you like along to an event like this – although it does have to be road legal and, if applicable, MoT'd.

I went along in a six-month-old Suzuki Jimny and thought I might feel rather 'out of it' being at the wheel of something so new; but not a bit of it. An even newer Ford Ranger double-cab truck was really being put through its paces, whilst the proud owner of an immaculate Series II

Discovery was clearly enjoying his first time at such an event. Short-wheelbase Land Rovers were out in force, of course; Series IIs mingled with Defenders, with even the odd Lightweight thrown in for good measure. And all of them were driven by people keen to uphold Land Rover's reputation as a world leader in the rough.

Long-wheelbase Land Rovers logically don't make such good off-roaders, if only because they're more likely to find themselves 'grounded'. But both a modified long-wheelbase Series III and a 110 Station Wagon were proving their critics wrong. In fact, with a whole family on board the 110, it was great to see parents and kids having such a laugh together.

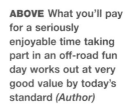

ABOVE What you'll pay for a seriously enjoyable time taking part in an off-road fun day works out at very good value by today's standard *(Author)*

OPPOSITE AND FAR LEFT Just about any competent 4x4 or SUV can take part in an off-road fun day, with original-shape Range Rovers being a popular budget buy among regular enthusiasts *(Author)*

LEFT You want off-road prowess? A 1990s Jeep Cherokee makes an interesting alternative to the evergreen products from downtown Solihull *(Author)*

The Japanese were well represented at Farley Quarry, with a modified Suzuki SJ in particular showing some of the bigger machinery just how it should be done. Apart, that is, from when it stalled in the lake and refused to start again for quite some time. Ah well, it's all part of the fun.

A short-wheelbase Isuzu Trooper also proved its mettle, powering its way up and over some fiercely steep and muddy inclines with ease, but it was a 1985 Daihatsu Fourtrak that seemed amongst the most unstoppable – despite being a relatively unmodified example of its type. In fact, so good are these old Daihatsus in the rough, this one was even called upon to tow an eight-wheel-drive amphibious vehicle from a particularly muddy small lake. The good-old Fourtrak performed this act of kindness with total ease … probably to the embarrassment of the driver of the 'amphi-vehicle'.

ABOVE You can always rely on a tough and rugged Daihatsu Fourtrak to get you out of trouble when the need arises! *(Author)*

BELOW A good old-fashioned workhorse, such as an Isuzu Trooper, makes an excellent part-time off-road machine, as well as providing perfectly adequate daily transport *(Author)*

With classic-shape Range Rovers and Series I Discoverys becoming so affordable these days, both models tend to be plentiful at most off-road events, and the activities at Much Wenlock proved why that is. Take any Range Rover or elderly Disco, treat it to a decent set of mud-plugging rubber and then just go and have fun. These old soldiers are so accomplished, they need virtually nothing doing to them in order to be some of the finest off-road machines that (not a lot of) money can buy. And the nice thing is that you can perform all these off-road antics in rather more comfort than the average old Series II Landie can offer – if such considerations are important to you.

If the products of Solihull don't appeal but you still want a practical, everyday 4x4 that's great off-road, how about the old-style Jeep Cherokee? With the earliest officially imported examples now getting on in years, their values have fallen significantly and they're now extremely affordable.

We had an absolute ball at Farley Quarry, and were impressed with just how well 'our' Suzuki Jimny coped with the tough terrain. Remember that whichever 4x4 you drive, there's a place for it at a fun day. If you simply want to potter around some of the less severe parts of a course, just to get a feel for what your vehicle is like off the road, then that's fine – and nobody will criticise you for it. And, of course, if you fancy being a touch more adventurous and really going for some of the more challenging sections, there are plenty of opportunities to do just that. The choice is yours – but either way, you're guaranteed to have great fun. It could well be what your 4x4 has been waiting for...

Go for it?

So, should you really consider taking your own 4x4 off-road in order to have a bit of fun? Many people do, and most of them love every minute of it. Just bear in mind that off-road damage can and will occur if you do this regularly, so you can certainly expect more frequent renewal of such items as alternators, batteries, brake pads and discs, steering boxes, suspension bushes and the like.

Most 4x4s are built for some degree of off-road activity, no matter how basic this may be. But regularly embarking upon it will take its toll in one way or another. Be careful, treat your vehicle and its surroundings with respect, enjoy yourself and you won't go far wrong. But just be aware that off-road damage is a fact of life. And don't forget to get your 4x4 back to clean and serviceable condition once you've finished playing; allow that old quarry mud to remain caked underneath indefinitely and you'll be heading for a whole range of vehicular ailments as a result, believe me.

Towing
the line

Market changes

Anybody experienced in towing caravans, trailers, boats or horseboxes will have witnessed a major shift in buying habits in recent times, with 4x4s being more popular than ever among the towing fraternity. Remember the days when caravans used to be hauled along behind standard saloons that struggled to make their way up motorway inclines without changing down a gear or two, inevitably causing massive tailbacks in the process?

Well, maybe that's a slight exaggeration. But the fact remains that no matter how powerful a good old-fashioned family saloon might be, towing a heavy caravan or boat is bound to put a strain on its suspension, steering and braking systems. And if its power output is only just adequate for the task in hand, it'll be doing untold long-term damage to the engine and transmission, too.

The change in buying habits really got under way in the 1980s when a selection of family-friendly, full-size 4x4s hit the market and provided the ideal solution for drivers with towing tasks to consider. The original Mitsubishi Shogun/Pajero and Isuzu Trooper arguably paved the way in the UK, joined at the end of the 1980s by the now legendary Land Rover Discovery. Subsequent launches from other manufacturers through the early 1990s and beyond (not least the Nissan Terrano II, Vauxhall Frontera and original Ford Maverick) suddenly gave buyers a greater choice than ever before.

What they could now buy was a reasonably large 4x4 that was not only powerful enough to be used every day and big enough to house the entire family, but one that would also tow heavy loads with far less effort than the conventional car that had preceded it. This new generation of 4x4 may not have provided the same kind of unstoppable off-road capabilities as a Land Rover Defender, but as perfectly practical and – for the time – surprisingly sophisticated everyday machines that would tow a family-size caravan with consummate ease, they excelled.

The benefits of a 4x4 family vehicle weren't confined to easier towing. With a caravan, after all, it's not just the actual towing process that's involved; there are also the family's belongings to stow away somewhere on board, as well as the kids, the dog and all manner of paraphernalia that's suddenly deemed essential for a fortnight's break in Cornwall or a spot of touring in the south of France. And it's a similar story with anybody who tows a boat behind them, for the towing vehicle itself invariably becomes the general holdall for the vast amount of equipment and supplies that are needed for a day on the water.

That's why you still see elderly Shoguns, Pajeros, Discoverys, Troopers, Terranos and the like giving superb service as towing vehicles and incredibly useful holdalls. Whatever the age of your well-proportioned 4x4, you'll find it genuinely capacious for the entire family, with a copious amount of luggage space bringing up the rear; and once a caravan or trailer is finally hitched behind, any such vehicle really comes into its own.

OPPOSITE A large proportion of 4x4s and SUVs – such as the Mitsubishi Shogun/Pajero – are now bought primarily for their excellence as towing vehicles, ideal for today's ever-growing band of caravanners *(Mitsubish)*

LEFT It's not just what a 4x4 is capable of towing that counts; it's also how much of the family's belongings it can swallow. The luggage area on this Toyota Land Cruiser is simply vast *(Author)*

The importance
of torque

The benefit of a larger-engined vehicle with tougher suspension and more in-built ruggedness than a conventional car seems pretty obvious when it comes to towing a heavy load. But why is all-wheel drive deemed essential? Well, if caravan holidays were always hot and dry, there'd be no real need for four-wheel traction. But as anybody who has been caravanning will testify, the usefulness of all-wheel drive when trying to drag your home-from-home through a muddy caravan site can be priceless. Even with standard road tyres fitted (as is the case with most family-owned 4x4s), it shouldn't be too difficult to remove a caravan from even the trickiest mud bath.

It's not just the four-wheel-drive aspect of most 4x4s that makes them such great towing vehicles. There's also – in the case of the majority of turbo-diesel versions – the impressive level of torque on offer; or, in simple terms, the amount of usable 'pulling power' that's being produced.

Diesel engines in general tend to produce higher torque outputs than their petrol equivalents – or at the very least, are able to provide similar torque figures from significantly smaller (and, by definition, more economical) powerplants. Early Land Rover Discovery V8s, for example, offered 192lb ft of torque from their 3528cc petrol engines, while the Tdi version managed 195lb ft from just a 2495cc four-cylinder unit. Just as important was that the V8's maximum torque was developed at 2800rpm compared with a mere 1800rpm with the Tdi. The lower down the rev range that maximum torque is developed, the more useful it is when off-roading or even when hauling a caravan around a muddy field.

When it comes to towing, there's an argument that low-down torque is far more important than

brake horsepower. Lots of torque when you're dragging a large caravan along the road makes for a more effortless driving experience, fewer gear changes, less strain on the engine and fewer problems when encountering steep hills or steady motorway inclines. The lower down the rev range the maximum torque is developed, the better it is in terms of usefulness; so, it would seem, something like an early Discovery 2.5 Tdi has just the right combination for the job.

OPPOSITE Double-cab 4x4 pick-ups are a popular alternative among the towing fraternity *(Mitsubishi)*

LEFT Full-size SUVs, such as the Land Rover Discovery, make superb towing vehicles and workhorses, and now offer superb value on the secondhand market *(Author)*

BELOW A turbo-diesel-powered SUV offers far more torque and beefier suspension than the average petrol-powered family estate; no wonder the caravan market is now dominated by 4x4s *(Author)*

Towing weights

Just as high torque levels help to reduce engine strain and driver frustrations, towing a trailer or caravan that's well within the maximum allowed for your vehicle will help to keep your 4x4 in good shape. What's the point of buying a car whose maximum towing weight only just exceeds the weight of your trailer or caravan, when you can spend the same money on a far more useful 4x4 that will do it with ease?

A word of warning before you buy any 4x4 likely to be used for towing a caravan: the issue of maximum towing weights isn't simply a case of quoting what's claimed by the manufacturer. In the UK in particular, the law is a little more complicated than that – and it falls on you, the driver, to make sure your vehicle and trailer/caravan combination is legal and acceptable.

First of all, you'll need to know your caravan's maximum technically permissible laden mass (MTPLM) if it was built in 1998 or later; if it's a pre-1998 caravan, you'll need to find out its maximum gross weight (MGW). You then need to know the kerb weight, nose weight and maximum towing limit for the specific 4x4 you intend towing with – and it has to be the exact model, as these do vary depending on wheelbase, engine choice and so on. You then need to ensure that your caravan's MTPLM does not exceed 85 per cent of your car's kerb weight; to do this, divide the actual laden weight of your caravan with the kerb weight of the towing vehicle, and then multiply by 100.

The closer the resultant figure gets to 85 per cent, the more difficult it is to tow. This is why it is recommended to buy a vehicle capable of towing far more than you intend, as it will make for a safer and more pleasant towing experience all round.

If all this is starting to sound rather complicated, don't worry. There's an organisation in the UK that will work out everything for you, based upon the make, model and year of both your towing vehicle and your caravan. Thanks to their unrivalled database of weights and specifications, they will be able to tell you almost immediately whether the 4x4 and caravan combination you're intending to purchase will be both safe and legal. They're called Towsafe and their website can be viewed at www.towsafe.co.uk.

I'd thoroughly recommend getting in touch with Towsafe and making use of their expertise. In most European countries these days, and particularly in the UK, illegal towing is taken very seriously. If a car/caravan outfit is incorrectly matched, British motorists can be looking at a substantial fine and three penalty points on their driving licence; taking any kind of a towing risk is both dangerous and illegal.

No wonder today's new and used family-size 4x4s are seen as such sensible choices for buyers who need to tow. With most promising extremely generous maximum towing weights according to their manufacturers, it would be difficult for many owners to haul around more than their vehicles were capable of. Even so,

it pays not to take any chances; confirmation from Towsafe (who will provide up to five checks for different combinations for a very reasonable registration fee) is surely money well spent.

One final point about towing, and it's all to do with your vehicle's actual towing bracket. In Britain, only towing brackets with official type approval should have been fitted since August 1st, 1998. Bear this in mind when buying a bracket – or, indeed, when buying any vehicle already fitted with a towing bracket. Are you completely confident your towing bracket is both safe and legal? If in any doubt, have a modern replacement professionally fitted without delay.

OPPOSITE What kind of vehicle will you need for hauling round a fully laden horsebox? Is your 4x4 powerful enough? Get your sums right because the legal implications are serious *(Nissan)*

LEFT Does your 4x4's towing bracket come with type approval? If fitted since 1998, it will need it. If in any doubt, don't take chances; have a new bracket fitted *(Author)*

BELOW Do you really know the maximum weight that your vehicle is capable of towing? Working it out can get complex, but help is at hand *(Isuzu)*

More research

Making sure that your 4x4 is big enough, powerful enough and heavy enough for whatever towing task you have in mind is absolutely essential. It's equally important that you carry out all the necessary research related to this before you buy either the caravan/trailer or the 4x4 of your choice.

Did you know, for example (assuming you're into extra-large caravans), that a caravan in excess of 2.3 metres in width or seven metres in length can be legally towed in the UK only by what's classed as a heavy motor vehicle – that is, one with a gross vehicle weight of more than 3500 kilograms? As the National Caravan Council (NCC) says on its website, 'Not even a Transit van, nor the biggest 4x4, can lawfully tow a caravan that exceeds these dimensions.'

Whether you're experienced at towing or a first-timer, it may well be worth getting hold of a copy of the NCC's excellent booklet: *The Caravan Towing Code*. It contains lots of recommendations reviewed and agreed by the Driving Standards Agency and is supported by both The Caravan Club and The Camping & Caravanning Club. You can obtain your own copy from any NCC dealer member or by emailing the NCC direct at: info@nationalcaravan.co.uk. It really does pay not to leave anything to chance.

Properly researching the art of towing and what your particular vehicle is capable of hauling around is essential these days. After all, by learning more about the kinds of caravans and trailers your vehicle can tow, as well as tips on actually driving with a caravan bringing up the rear, you can do a lot to prevent unnecessary strain on your vehicle and any kind of resultant damage. It's not just a legal issue; it also has a great deal to do with treating your 4x4 well and ensuring it has many years of hard-working reliability ahead of it.

The NCC is also able to offer essential information on the best way to load a caravan, the advantages of stabilisers, how breakaway cables work, looking after your caravan's wheels and tyres and a whole lot more. Any such advice that helps you to make your caravan-towing experience safer and more pleasurable will also have a positive effect on your vehicle and its long-term condition. Check out the NCC's website for the full rundown: www.nationalcaravan.co.uk.

RIGHT Planning on towing a trailer? *The Trailer Manual* from Haynes will tell you all you need to know *(Haynes)*

OPPOSITE Whatever you're intending to tow, it pays to get all the advice and help you need before you actually take to the road for the first time *(SsangYong)*

LEFT There's plenty of reading material for the first-time caravanner these days, including Haynes Publishing's excellent *The Caravan Handbook (Haynes)*

Added security

Anybody new to the world of towing in general and touring caravans in particular will probably be impressed with the level of information and assistance available through various official organisations. The best news of all, though, is that when you need it most, even more help is out there – not least when it comes to the safety and security of your caravan.

Although it has little to do with actual towing advice, it's worth mentioning here the excellent services provided by the Caravan Registration & Identification Scheme (CRiS), a system that operates for caravans in a similar way that the DVLA does for cars. It provides you with the benefit of a registration document and record of ownership for your caravan, as well as maintaining information relating to any interest in a caravan held by finance and insurance companies.

All new caravans built by member companies of the National Caravan Council not only feature a unique 17-digit CRiS vehicle identification number (VIN) die-stamped onto the chassis, but their windows are also etched with the VIN and an electronic tag is embedded into the bodywork for extra security.

All of this enables you to make various checks before buying any used caravan (all models built since 1992 should come with their own CRiS registration document), thus providing unique peace of mind. Simply call CRiS (on 01722 411430), tell them the VIN of the caravan you're thinking of buying and, for a very small fee, they'll be able to tell you almost instantly whether it has ever been reported as stolen, written-off by an insurance company or is still subject to outstanding finance.

Caravan thefts aren't uncommon, but thanks to efforts made by both the NCC and CRiS there's now a great deal more that can be done to deter thieves and keep your caravan safe and sound.

Safety first

Your personal well-being and the safety of other road users are equally important points to consider – particularly if you're the first-time owner of a caravan or you're inexperienced when towing. It all starts with the basics of coupling your caravan to your 4x4. Fortunately, the NCC has prepared a leaflet (accessible via the organisation's website) on this very subject, offering sound and sensible advice on how to couple-up your 4x4 and caravan combination. There are seven basic steps to follow, as well as a nine-point checklist; and although some of the advice may seem obvious, it's vital that you follow it and develop a strict routine when planning to tow any caravan, trailer, boat or horsebox. The advice is there for your benefit – follow it closely and you won't go far wrong.

Of course, there's the matter of your driving techniques to consider, too. No matter how safe your caravan and 4x4 combination may seem, they can only be described as such if there's a competent and experienced driver at the wheel. So if you're new to the world of towing or you haven't done any for a few years, I'd strongly recommend that you embark upon a professional training or refresher course without delay. Just because your driving licence permits you to drive a 4x4 that's towing a caravan doesn't mean you don't have more to learn on the subject.

Take your towing seriously, get the right training and make sure your 4x4 and trailer combination is a safe one. You can't be too careful. With so much help and advice so easily at hand, there's really no excuse for not getting it right these days. It's by far the best way of ensuring many years of happy – and safe – holidays ahead for you, your family and your 4x4.

OPPOSITE If you're buying a new caravan, the Caravan Registration & Identification Scheme (CRiS) provides both security and peace of mind *(Subaru)*

ABOVE Buying a used caravan? you can now check whether it's ever been stolen *(Subaru)*

BELOW If you're new to towing or you haven't done it for many years, have you considered professional training? It could make life a lot easier – and safer *(Mitsubishi)*

The
crossovers

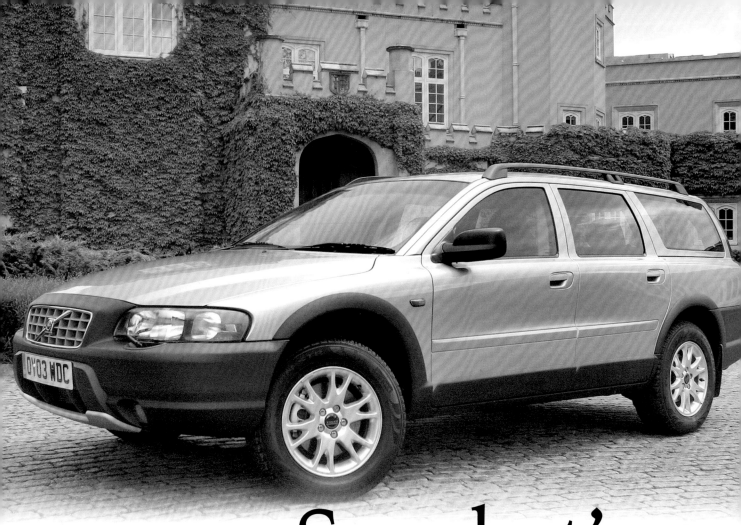

So what's a crossover?

If the general car market has fragmented and diversified since the end of the 1980s, then the 4x4 scene has also been following suit. No longer is a 4x4 simply an off-road vehicle for those who need all-wheel traction; it's also a style statement aimed as much at the urban crowd as rural dwellers. And in any sector of the market where fashion, style and mixed requirements are the order of the day, it's inevitable that different manufacturers will choose to go in different directions.

So we have a 4x4 scene and new-vehicle market where all-wheel-drive estate cars with butched-up styling and little real off-road ability mix happily with proper SUVs and rough-stuff workhorses. Which kind of vehicle appeals to you most will depend not just on your personal requirements but also on your style preferences, which is why we've split the scene into different categories for the next few chapters. It will enable you to get a feel for what's around, both new and secondhand, as well as comparing both obvious rivals and cross-class alternatives.

There has been a gradual blurring of the edges between different sectors of the 4x4 scene over the years, with several manufacturers insisting

their 4x4s are proper sports utility vehicles while much of the motoring press refers to them as soft-roaders. Who is right? Well, that's debatable, and you may come across listings of models in different sectors here that you may not actually agree with. But … well, that's partly what makes the whole 4x4 scene so interesting.

Soft-roaders, SUVs and 4x4 workhorses will be dealt with in depth over the next few chapters. Before that, there's the more straightforward subject of crossovers to consider.

In simple terms, a crossover is a 4x4 that's based upon – or at least heavily related to – a straightforward road-going two-wheel-drive machine, which in most cases means an estate car. Most crossovers come with permanent four-wheel drive, although they usually lack the dual-range transfer box associated more with the world of SUVs. Styling-wise, they tend to be a bit of a mixed bag, ranging from those that look almost identical to their standard donor models to those which ooze masculinity thanks to their add-on plastic embellishments, raised ride height and ever-ready image.

Unsurprisingly, there's been no shortage of crossover 4x4s launched over the years, and the sector is very much alive and well nowadays. But why would anybody choose a crossover instead of an SUV or a proper off-roader?

Well, with its lower-slung car-based styling, a crossover 4x4 tends to be a better-handling machine than a good many 'proper' off-roaders and, for anybody covering a high annual mileage or who likes to drive enthusiastically, that can be a real plus point. They often offer better value too, as you're essentially buying a standard machine that happens to have all-wheel drive rather than an out and out off-road special or hyped-up SUV. But remember, if you've previously been used to, say, a Land Rover Discovery and you decide to opt for one of the more popular crossovers instead, you may well find yourself missing the high-up driving position, panoramic view and the great feeling of invincibility that a full-size SUV can bring.

Basing a crossover on an estate is a logical move, as the latter was often historically marketed as a lifestyle vehicle anyway. As far back as the 1930s, estates were known as shooting brakes, designed to appeal to the rural gentry with their hunting, shooting and fishing activities. Who could forget such lifestyle-based monikers for estate cars as Austin's Countryman and Morris's Traveller models from the 1950s onwards? In many ways, the creation of the crossover much later on was merely an extension of such a theme.

Not every crossover is based upon a standard estate car, of course – and today's smallest offerings are proof of this. The 2004-onwards Fiat Panda 4x4 has its roots in one of Europe's smallest city cars, while the Renault Kangoo Trekka is very obviously van-based – but is none the worse for that. I've also included in this section such models as the Subaru Forester and Legacy, neither of which is available in Europe in anything other than 4x4 guise – but I'll explain more about that further on.

From a manufacturer's point of view, launching a crossover makes serious economic sense, as it enables an extra model to be added to the company's line-up with relatively little expenditure. Similarly, it brings a 4x4 to the range without the massive development costs involved in creating a brand new SUV from scratch. And while overall sales may not come close to matching what could be achieved with a class-beating SUV or soft-roader, the existence of a crossover gives a useful boost to any company's overall sales figures – and image, of course.

The good news is that most new-and-used-car budgets these days will stretch to a crossover of some description. The bad news is that it may not be the sexy, head-turning vehicle you were hoping for.

OPPOSITE If you want a 4x4, you don't have to consider an all-conquering SUV. A new or used all-wheel-drive crossover estate is now an ideal choice for increasing numbers of buyers *(Volvo)*

TOP LEFT The crossover market has seen many success stories over the years, attracting buyers who demand a car-like driving experience coupled with more rugged capabilities than the average family transport *(Subaru)*

BELOW At the bottom end of the crossover market comes the Fiat Panda 4x4, a surprisingly capable machine based on little more than a standard supermini *(Fiat)*

Cheap and **cheerful**

Those with restricted budgets can't always get what they dream of. What they can get, though, is an elderly crossover vehicle for a pretty insignificant sum.

At the bottom of the scale size-wise (and in terms of desirability, too) come the original 1980s Fiat Panda and Subaru Justy models, each offering minuscule proportions and part-time all-wheel drive. Most examples will long since have been scrapped, though rare survivors can make an interesting budget buy.

Subaru's Justy grew up somewhat in the mid-1990s when a new-generation model was introduced. In reality, this was little more than a Hungarian-built four-wheel-drive version of the already elderly Suzuki Swift (bizarre but true), which meant its chances of serious sales success in Europe would always be limited.

If an elderly Subaru appeals to you, far better instead to invest a relatively small amount of cash in an original-style Subaru Legacy Estate, an all-wheel-drive capacious estate that's reliable, durable and sounds great too, thanks to the company's legendary flat-four 'boxer' engine.

Further up the price ladder come more recent crossovers, as it wasn't until the late 1990s that this sector of the 4x4 market really began to expand. But bargains are still there to be had, with Volvo in particular providing several temptations. Remember the old 850 estate, the load-lugging version of Volvo's first ever front-wheel-drive design? By the time it ceased production in 1997, it was being produced in four-wheel-drive AWD guise and was proving something of a hit. So much so that its mildly restyled successor, the V70, subsequently became available in four-wheel-drive form, known as the AWD or XC. It was the XC that proved particularly interesting, using the same 4x4 driveline as the AWD but with an increased ride height and a whole raft of plastic styling add-ons to give it a semi-SUV character all of its own. 4x4 traditionalists may not have truly understood the XC's concept, but for estate car fans it was an exciting newcomer with enormous potential.

Nowadays, a secondhand V70 AWD or V70 XC makes an excellent buy for anybody looking

for space, roadholding, toughness and all-round practicality. It's a luxury car too, with a price tag which reflects this. Look at how little you'll be expected to pay for an elderly example now and you should be very pleasantly surprised.

Even the V70 XC, of course, is no off-roader in the true sense of the term – despite its raised suspension and four-wheel drive compared with standard versions. But that doesn't mean it has no off-road prowess at all, for it will prove a formidable challenger when it comes to towing a caravan across a muddy field or a horsebox across a slippery stable yard. What you expect your 4x4 to do away from the tarmac will affect whether or not a crossover like the V70 will actually fulfil your needs.

OPPOSITE A completely redesigned Justy arrived in 1997, even though it was little more than the existing Suzuki Swift fitted with all-wheel drive. The ultimate in cheap and cheerful crossovers? *(Subaru)*

LEFT Crossovers don't come much cheaper or more basic than this! The original 1980s Fiat Panda 4x4 is a bargain-basement buy – if you can find a good one *(Author)*

BELOW Would you consider a used Volvo 850 AWD over the more popular Land Rover Freelander or any other soft-roader? Plenty of buyers would *(Author)*

German
challengers

Assuming the Volvo V70 AWD is on your used-car shopping list, you'll be well advised also to consider some all-wheel-drive challengers from Germany, particularly 4x4 versions of the Audi A4 and A6 Avant (estate). Famously carrying the quattro name tag, any four-wheel-drive Audi combines class-leading levels of on-road handling, roadholding and driver feedback with typically Germanic build quality and long-term reliability. But it's the Audi A6 Avant-based allroad quattro that particularly interests us here.

Launched in most markets in 2000, the allroad quattro took its influence from the Volvo V70 XC, combining a 4x4 drivetrain with pseudo-off-road looks and an uprated suspension system – in this case an adaptive air-suspension set-up that enables the car to hug the road at speed or to enjoy soft-roader-type ground clearance when the need arises.

Like its Volvo rival, the allroad quattro may not be the kind of off-roader in which to tackle the Paris–Dakar Rally, but as a hugely useful all-wheel-drive machine for real-world motoring it's absolutely ideal. As its name suggests, it's one of the finest devices for coping with just about any road or track that lies in its path.

Turning
Japanese

Perhaps not surprisingly, it took a Japanese company to master the art of the crossover vehicle long before the Volvo XC and Audi allroad were even thought of. That company goes by the name of Subaru.

These days, motoring fanatics tend to associate Subaru with rally-winning successes thanks to the all-conquering capabilities of the legendary Impreza Turbo super-saloon. But the brand is also the most successful manufacturer of niche crossover vehicles you're likely to find anywhere – which means lots of opportunities for the secondhand-car buyer.

ABOVE AND BELOW Based on the Impreza platform, the boxy-looking Forester has attracted a loyal following over the years – and justifiably so *(Subaru)*

The most practical of the Subaru crossovers has to be the Forester, a uniquely styled five-door estate that's not available in any other guise than the crossover versions we're familiar with. What makes it a crossover rather than a soft-roader is that it employs essentially the same floorpan, running gear and engines as the more mainstream versions of the Impreza line-up, albeit clad with a boxier, more workmanlike bodyshell. It's a recipe that works brilliantly, for the Forester's combination of extra ground clearance, practical styling, tough image and unrivalled reliability has won it many friends over the years.

Most European-market Subaru Foresters have traditionally come with normally-aspirated 2.0-litre 'boxer' power, though turbocharged versions have also proved tempting for those buyers who want a crossover with serious tarmac-ripping performance.

What makes the Forester really stand out from the crowd is that this all-wheel-drive crossover comes with SUV-like dual-range gearing for extra

ABOVE The Legacy was seriously restyled for the 21st century, with the more rugged Outback, in particular, looking superb. The main downside was the lack of a diesel-engine option *(Subaru)*

BELOW With revised styling, extra equipment and a larger range of powerplants, the Forester estate had evolved into an even more tempting choice by 2005 *(Subaru)*

potential when out in the rough. Again, this isn't the kind of vehicle to get you to the same places as a Land Rover Defender or Jeep Wrangler; but compared with most other crossovers, the Forester has real off-road potential.

For those who demand a larger Subaru, of course, there's always the four-wheel-drive Legacy Estate, a model that has proved a firm favourite in various different guises and through several restyles over the years. But for crossover admirers, it's the Legacy Outback that's of particular interest, an upmarket semi-off-roader with a unique-in-its-class flat-six petrol engine and more on-board equipment than a luxury liner (well, almost). It offers greater ground clearance than a regular Legacy Estate, although it has avoided the pseudo-SUV styling add-ons so favoured by its true rivals from Volvo and Audi.

Would we recommend the Legacy Outback? Most certainly. But, as with the Forester, there's never been a diesel option in the line-up (so far, that is) – which means that budget-conscious secondhand buyers might be deterred.

Subaru hasn't been the only Japanese company to enter the all-important crossover market over the years, of course. In the 1980s there was the fairly uninspiring Tercel 4WD Estate from Toyota, while Honda tried to tempt buyers with its Civic Shuttle 4x4. Even though neither model set European markets alight with its sales success, each proved a useful introduction to the crossover as a concept.

ABOVE The Forester may look like a perfectly ordinary estate car inside – but what's so wrong with that? It offers just the right amount of practicality for most families *(Subaru)*

The newcomers

The new-car market of the last few years has seen scores of new crossover vehicles launched, all aimed at grabbing a piece of the non-SUV all-wheel-drive action. It's a market that covers an astonishingly wide spread of styles and price ranges.

At the bottom of the pile price-wise is the latest Fiat Panda 4x4 mentioned earlier on in this chapter, a cheeky little chappy that manages to combine an exceptionally keen list price with a foolproof all-wheel-drive set-up. This clever but straightforward bit of kit sees the Panda using front-wheel drive for normal road use, with a viscous coupling taking additional drive to the rear wheels when the fronts begin to struggle or over-spin. It's fully automatic, it requires no input whatsoever from the driver and it's all surprisingly effective. Admittedly, the Panda 4x4 lacks the ground clearance and ultimate go-anywhere ability of a miniature SUV (like the Suzuki Jimny), but that's fine; as a cut-price crossover, it truly excels.

The other truly affordable-when-new crossover vehicle comes from France, in the shape of the Renault Kangoo Trekka. Based on the regular Kangoo hatchback, which in turn is a thinly disguised Kangoo van fitted with windows, the Trekka has fairly utilitarian roots, but it still manages to offer a terrific driving style, with eager performance, excellent handling and a surprisingly smooth ride all in its favour. Like the Panda, it uses a viscous coupling to take power to the rear wheels when it's needed, but the Renault also comes with front-wheel traction control for even more reassurance. At its best in diesel guise, the Kangoo Trekka is affordable, likeable and makes a superb holdall for any family. Ignore it at your peril.

Further up the new-car price range comes a wider choice of crossovers from other manufacturers, with such models as the latest Subaru Forester and Legacy Outback, the Volvo XC70 and the uniquely styled (but technologically Shogun/Pajero-influenced) Mitsubishi Outlander all providing tempting reasons to buy them. Meanwhile, for those who simply demand an all-wheel-drive estate without the image of an off-road lookalike, 4x4 versions of the Mazda 6 Estate and latest Skoda Octavia Estate are also available.

Estate or crossover?

It's a fine line that divides an 'ordinary' estate that happens to be four-wheel drive and a crossover vehicle that boasts extra ground clearance, a tougher image and semi-off-road capabilities. But it's an important difference to mention.

As far back as the 1980s, for example, Ford dabbled in the all-wheel-drive estate market with the Sierra 4x4, a model with handling and roadholding like that of no other Sierra Estate before. But to call it a crossover vehicle would perhaps be taking things a step too far; the Sierra's emphasis was very much on tarmac-based all-wheel traction rather than any pretence at being a farmer's friend.

The 21st century, though, has seen Ford re-entering the European 4x4 estate car market with

the highly successful Jaguar X-Type, a far more road-biased machine than many of its current rivals. But we mention it here with good reason.

The X-Type may not boast the same kind of semi-off-road image as the Audi allroad quattro, but that hasn't stopped Jaguar referring to it as a 'winter sports' car – which means it's very much a lifestyle vehicle, particularly among the ski and snowboard crowd that Jaguar focuses on in its promotions of the model. So although the V6-engined Jaguar X-Type all-wheel drive may look like a rather smart but otherwise standard estate car, its underpinnings and marketing suggest far more of a lifestyle/activity approach than that. Perhaps Jaguar should be congratulated on pulling off such a clever feat.

OPPOSITE In today's fairly bland new-car market, the arrival of such affordable niche models as the Panda 4x4 is guaranteed to put a smile on every owner's face *(Fiat)*

ABOVE Another all-wheel-drive estate worthy of consideration is the Mitsubishi Outlander, an oddly styled but perfectly capable addition to the crossover class *(Mitsubishi)*

BELOW Can the all-wheel-drive Jaguar X-Type Estate be considered a true crossover? Its maker markets it as a 'winter sports' lifestyle car – so why not? *(Jaguar)*

Something
different

Mention of the Skoda marque earlier brings to mind a few (very)
different alternatives for those seeking a secondhand crossover,
as the original-style Octavia Estate was available in various all-
wheel-drive versions from the end of 2000. Offering permanent
four-wheel drive and super on-road grip, this was a highly
competent estate car and now represents fantastic value for
money on the secondhand market. From a technical and styling
point of view, the old-style Octavia is like many other estate cars
on the market, but the exceptional value offered by its Skoda
badge marks it out as something different nowadays.

Not different enough for you? Then you might consider going 'grey', opting for an unofficially imported Japanese crossover based on an MPV instead. That's where the Mitsubishi Delica and Mazda Bongo come into their own, each offering multi-seat convenience combined with all-wheel-drive traction. The Mazda derivative is even available in various camper guises for what is arguably the ultimate in leisure and lifestyle vehicles. If that's the kind of thing that gets your imagination working overtime, contact your nearest specialist 'grey' importer and see what deals are available in your area.

The crossover concept encompasses so many different sizes, designs, types and values of vehicles, it's just about as diverse as it can be. But that doesn't necessarily mean there's one here that's ideal for you. It's essential you weigh up the car-like convenience and driving style of most models against their ultimate lack of off-road capabilities before you take the plunge. If this is the right kind of vehicle for you, there are some great choices available. If not, maybe you need something just that bit more competent when the going gets tough(er)?

OPPOSITE For something truly different from the norm, how about a 'grey' import crossover in the unlikely shape of the Mitsubishi Delica Spacegear… *(Author)*

ABOVE …or the ludicrously-named Mazda Bongo? Both offer what is arguably the ultimate solution to today's quest for 'leisure vehicles' *(Author)*

BELOW For one of the best secondhand crossovers on a tight budget, you'll be well advised not to ignore the original-shape Skoda Octavia 4x4 – a well-built and reliable offering *(Skoda)*

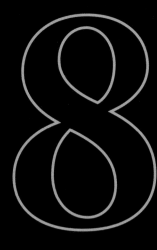

The soft-roader

Another new idea

The term soft-roader can trace its roots back to the launch of the original Toyota RAV4 in 1994, although the Japanese company probably had little idea back then just what a revolution it was single-handedly creating. After all, this was a time when even the most compact 4x4s were usually more than capable of heading off-road when the need arose. Up until then, the likes of Suzuki's SJ, Samurai and Vitara ranges were all 'proper' SUVs, each a with separate chassis, a dual-range transfer box and genuine off-road capabilities. They were compromised when out on the road, of course, but surely that didn't matter to buyers of affordable 4x4s? Toyota, it seems, thought it did.

Hence the arrival of the RAV4, a brand new 4x4 that was actually a very fine road car, too. With its monocoque construction and permanent all-wheel drive, it was more modern than any compact all-wheel drive before it, and with a high-revving 2.0-litre 16-valve petrol engine providing the power, the RAV4 was a faster, more road-biased 4x4 than just about anything else in its class.

Except, of course, it was difficult deciding which 'rivals' were actually in the same class as Toyota's newcomer. Here was a 4x4 that behaved more like a hot hatch, so where was its natural competition? Some way behind, is the obvious answer.

Not everybody understood the concept of the Toyota RAV4 straight away, but rival companies such as Land Rover were intrigued by the newcomer. Indeed, Land Rover – then part of the Rover Group – had been working on the idea of a compact 'lifestyle' car themselves, a model that (it was thought) would eventually be launched in both Rover and Land Rover guises, the latter being the version with all-wheel drive. But by the time development of what was to become the Freelander got officially under way in 1994, the plans had changed – and that can no doubt be attributed in part to the arrival of the RAV4, which had been unveiled in prototype form the previous year.

For Land Rover traditionalists, the idea of the Solihull marque creating a rival to the Toyota RAV4 was sacrilege. Land Rover was all about world-beating off-road machines, after all. What business did it have meddling in what would soon become known as the soft-roader section of the market?

With the benefit of hindsight, of course, it can be seen that the decision to develop the Freelander was one of the best ever made by the management at Land Rover, for the newcomer would go on to become Europe's best-selling 4x4 within a year of its launch in 1998. Its arrival also meant a major expansion of the soft-roader sector, a part of the 4x4 market that is now one of the most thriving and successful.

Cynics may have scoffed when the first soft-roaders hit the streets. But, as was soon to become obvious, this was exactly the kind of 4x4 that a large proportion of potential buyers genuinely wanted. And it wasn't long before they were voting with their wallets.

OPPOSITE The original Toyota RAV4 was largely responsible for the creation of the soft-roader class. *(Toyota)*

ABOVE The ultimate in Land Rover lifestyle vehicles? Probably, even though the Freelander Softback was very much a niche product *(Land Rover)*

LEFT Even before the RAV4 came along, the Rover Group had been toying with the idea of a compact new leisure vehicle; the result was the Land Rover Freelander *(Land Rover)*

What makes a soft-roader?

As mentioned in chapter seven, the boundaries between different sectors of the 4x4 market can become slightly blurred as numerous models come and go, leaving their influence behind them. But in general, it's fairly straightforward sorting the soft-roaders of today from the genuine SUVs.

In many (but not all) cases, for example, a soft-roader will boast monocoque construction rather than offering a separate backbone chassis. It will often lack a dual-range transfer box too, although whether it offers pearmanent or part-time four-wheel drive varies from model to model. But what every soft-roader does without exception is put more emphasis on its road-going characteristics than it does on any pretence to be a world-beating off-roader.

That doesn't mean, of course, that a soft-roader can't go off-road. In fact, a model such as the Freelander – with its electronic traction control, hill descent control and decent suspension travel – will prove quite a formidable contender in some off-road situations. But that's seen by most buyers as a bonus, for in every other respect the Freelander is very much a soft-roader. And that's where its (and its rivals') emphasis will always be.

Since the arrival of the original Toyota RAV4, the soft-roader section has expanded at an unprecedented rate, and now it's one of the most hotly contested throughout Europe and beyond. Soft-roaders come in many different sizes, to varying levels of specification and at all different price levels – from the most humble Daihatsu Terios to the most tempting BMW X3. And once the secondhand market is taken into account, you'll find most 4x4 buyers' budgets will now stretch to a soft-roader of some description. But which ones should be most seriously considered by those intent on entering the soft-roader scene?

OPPOSITE It's not that soft-roaders can't go off-road, as this 2000-model Freelander happily proves; it's just that on-tarmac progress is deemed more important *(Land Rover)*

ABOVE Is this the most outrageously styled soft-roader ever to make it into production? Whatever you think of its looks, the Nissan Murano is certainly different *(Nissan)*

BELOW The 1994-2000 Toyota RAV4 became a phenomenally popular choice throughout Europe, appealing to 4x4 buyers who appreciated best-in-class performance and handling *(Toyota)*

ABOVE Sharing its underpinnings and powerplants with the Tucson is the Kia Sportage, a drastically different vehicle from its predecessor of the same name *(Kia)*

Used or abused?

If funds are limited and you find yourself in the market for a secondhand soft-roader, there are a few points to bear in mind. Firstly, although very few soft-roaders ever experience regular life in the rough, they can suffer from lifestyle damage in other ways – not least the battle scars left behind by children, pets and heavy loads being hauled around in daily use. Secondly, you should realise that because soft-roaders tend to be used as daily family transport far more than any Land Rover Defender ever will, they're likely to have covered higher mileages than some 4x4 buyers might expect. And, lastly, you need to take a long look at your available budget and decide in advance whether you wish to opt for something older but still tempting like an early-shape Toyota RAV4 or something newer but smaller like a Daihatsu Terios – both of which will cost roughly the same kind of money.

With the soft-roader sector of the market having been around for quite some time now, you'll find a massive range of asking prices out there for secondhand examples, with the earliest (circa 1997) versions of the Daihatsu Terios, for example, now being available in most markets for relatively little cash. This diminutive five-door model looks oddly tall and narrow from some angles, but is still a genuine four-seater with a reasonable boot – and is as reliable and dependable as its maker's name tends to suggest. Later examples powered by the Toyota Yaris engine are the best, though just about any 1.3-litre petrol-powered Terios will perform the role of budget-priced soft-roader with ease.

It's the fact that the Terios (with its permanent four-wheel drive) lacks the similarly-priced Suzuki Jimny's dual-range transfer box that dictates its position as a soft-roader rather than an SUV. And it's not alone in that. Both the Series I (1994–2000) and Series II (2000–2006) versions of the Toyota RAV4 fall into the same category, their permanent all-wheel drive doing nothing to counteract the almost total lack of concession to any kind of off-road kit. That's because the RAV4 was engineered to be the best-handling, best-performing 4x4 of its price on the road – something it achieved from the start; and on the road is where it truly belongs.

Rather like most crossovers and soft-roaders, a RAV4 will happily take you (and your caravan or trailer if necessary) up a rough track or along the nearest beach with few problems. But ask it to tackle anything more challenging and it will encounter difficulties. Is that a problem? Not if you value on-road behaviour and performance over and above any kind of off-road prowess. If you're in the market for a soft-roader in the first place, I'm assuming that's the case.

Despite the age of the earliest RAV4s, this model still has a superb reputation for overall reliability, something that can't be said for its British arch rival, the Land Rover Freelander. Although Freelander quality and reliability have improved during its production life, secondhand examples still have a reputation for fragility compared with their Japanese opposition. But that doesn't stop the Freelander having a loyal and enthusiastic following, not just in the UK but further afield, too.

Compared with most soft-roader rivals, the Freelander is impressively competent as an off-road machine, as well as also being a likeable on-road experience. The most popular (and most convenient) have always been the five-door models, known as the Station Wagon, and the best engine choice in later years was arguably BMW's Td4 unit. Mind you, there's a lot to be said for the power and effortless feel of a secondhand Freelander V6, although its heavier fuel consumption will deter many potential buyers from the experience.

A large proportion of Freelanders, though, have found themselves fitted with the ex-Rover 1.8-litre K-series petrol engine, a unit with a reputation for premature head gasket failure – as explained in Chapter Four. It's important to make yourself aware of an individual soft-roader's weak points before you venture into the used-4x4 minefield.

OPPOSITE Although soft-roaders rarely experience off-road damage, their interiors can suffer from the daily abuse inflicted on most 'school run' cars *(Toyota)*

BELOW Like its predecessor, the second-generation RAV4 was available in three- and five-door guises, though a wider choice of engines was now available *(Toyota)*

Success for
Honda

A major rival to both the Freelander and the RAV4 since the late 1990s has been the Honda CR-V, an attractive and successful five-door soft-roader with styling not dissimilar to Land Rover's smallest offering. Early examples with their standard 2.0-litre petrol engine weren't as fast or as much fun to pilot as a RAV4, but the Honda gained points for its cleverly designed interior, its superb build quality and its pleasing driving style.

When the second-generation CR-V arrived in 2002, it was instantly recognisable as the original's replacement, thanks to its evolutionary rather than revolutionary styling. Worthwhile improvements have included the arrival of a turbo-diesel engine option, as well as a 150bhp V-TEC petrol unit.

All-wheel drive was provided courtesy of a clever central clutch set-up, providing drive to the rear wheels once the front ones began to spin. For soft-roader fans who didn't want the driveline drag and poorer economy usually associated with permanent four-wheel drive, and who found selecting all-wheel drive manually way too much trouble, such a set-up was ideal.

Both generations of CR-V provide a tempting choice on the used car market these days. But if you crave something a bit more fun and funky from your soft-roader budget, Honda has an alternative in the shape of the smaller, more angular HR-V. It may not have proved such a top-selling soft-roader as its bigger brother, but the oh-so-distinctive HR-V is a favourite choice among younger buyers.

Honda's original description of the HR-V as The Joy Machine may have been a bit over the top, but this was – and still is – a genuinely fun product. And it arguably comes closer to defining the soft-roader concept than almost anything else in its class.

First is the HR-V's styling: dramatic and different with its steeply sloping front end, glassy cabin and sharply cut-off rear. It looks by far the best in three-door guise, but any HR-V will stand out in a crowd like few other 4x4s – at any price.

Not every HRV came with four-wheel drive, and even those that did were hardly extreme off-roaders – but that wasn't the point. These 1.6-litre petrol-engined funsters gave good performance, decent handling and room for four adults, combined with the kind of head-turning looks guaranteed to attract attention in the city. The HR-V may not be the first choice soft-roader for everyone, but for fans of the model it's a mini marvel.

OPPOSITE By the time the Series II CR-V arrived in 2002, Honda's most popular 4x4 was a more sophisticated and even more tempting offering in the soft-roader class *(Honda)*

ABOVE You want a 4x4 that's fun, funky and affordable? The Honda HR-V is a likeable machine, even if its off-road capabilities are severely restricted *(Honda)*

BELOW The second-generation Honda CR-V is remarkably similar to the Freelander in style and concept, and a number are used by the ambulance services *(Honda)*

New arrivals

Although the soft-roader class began a rapid expansion from the mid-1990s onwards, it wasn't until the beginning of the 21st century that some of the world's most important manufacturers began entering the sector in earnest.

Nissan, in particular, had for a long time been a successful producer of 4x4s, but it wasn't until the arrival of the X-Trail model in 2001 that the company deemed it necessary to have a soft-roader in its line-up. It complemented the Terrano II and Patrol SUVs that sat further up the range, and finally gave Nissan a strong product with which to take on the Freelander, RAV4 and CR-V.

If better-than-average off-road capabilities are important in your soft-roader, the X-Trail might just be the vehicle for you, rivalling as it does the prowess of the Freelander when out in the rough. The X-Trail will switch automatically from front- to four-wheel drive when the need arises, but this transition can also be done manually if the driver prefers. It's this ability to manually lock the X-Trail's all-wheel-drive setting that marks it out as unusual in the soft-roader class.

The X-Trail is a handsome machine, too, and manages to combine excellent on-road characteristics with the kind of comfort, convenience and quality that buyers of Japanese models have come to expect. A choice of 2.0- or 2.5-litre petrol engines and a 2.2-litre direct-injection turbo-diesel unit help ensure there's an X-Trail to suit most tastes and driving styles.

It's little wonder Nissan has enjoyed major success with the X-Trail, despite its being up against some very impressive rivals. And, as with other sectors of the new-car market these days, much of that competition now comes from Korea.

It was with the launch of the Hyundai Santa Fe in 2000 that the Koreans started taking the soft-roader market seriously, for here was a distinctively styled five-door 4x4 with permanent all-wheel drive, lots of equipment and a very tempting range of prices. The sole engine choice to begin with was a 2.4-litre four-cylinder that proved both lacklustre and uneconomical, though the subsequent arrival of a 2.7-litre V6 and a 2.0-litre turbo diesel answered both such criticisms in turn. And, not surprisingly, it didn't take long for the Santa Fe to catch on among European buyers looking for a high-spec package and a superb warranty at a highly affordable price.

Not everyone will appreciate the Santa Fe's curvaceous looks, nor the relatively crude ride (despite the Hyundai's all-independent suspension), but as a soft-roader that will go most places its rivals can, and almost certainly with utter reliability and dependability, it's just too good a proposition to ignore – whether you're thinking of buying new or secondhand.

The success of the Santa Fe led Hyundai to develop a smaller, cheaper model with which to take on the bottom end of the soft-roader market, hence the arrival of the new Tucson in 2004. Again, this compact and distinctive newcomer has proved a seriously tempting proposition for budget-conscious buyers.

The Tucson may lack the Santa Fe's permanent all-wheel drive, but its auto-engaging 4x4 set-up is more than adequate for most buyers' needs. The fact that it employs front-drive only for normal road use obviously helps to improve fuel consumption, too – which for a model aimed mainly at urban dwellers is a major consideration.

With a choice of 2.0-litre petrol or turbo-diesel engines, not to mention the Santa Fe's 2.7-litre V6, there's no shortage of options for the Tucson buyer. In fairness, that V6 isn't ideally suited to such a compact soft-roader; far better instead to opt for the turbo diesel and enjoy all the fuel economy benefits it brings.

Models such as the Tucson aren't without competition, of course, though its main rival actually comes from within the same company. Kia, itself part of the mighty Hyundai empire, re-launched its compact Sportage in 2004, although the newcomer was a world away from the fairly basic and dated SUV of the same name that had gone before. Suddenly, the brand new Sportage was a stylish soft-roader, sharing a similar engine range (and auto-engaging four-wheel drive) as its Tucson stablemate. Off-road antics were feasible too, thanks to the Sportage's electronic traction control – even if, as with most soft-roaders, this meant easy traversing of rough tracks rather than any kind of serious mountain climbing.

OPPOSITE Unlike some of its soft-roader contemporaries, the X-Trail is a fairly accomplished off-roader, as Nissan was keen to prove from the start *(Nissan)*

LEFT The success of the Santa Fe led Hyundai to add a smaller, less expensive soft-roader to the range in 2004 in the shape of the Tucson *(Hyundai)*

More upmarket

As demand for soft-roaders has increased over the years, so has the size of the sector itself, which has generated a range of soft-roader designs that are more expensive and upmarket than ever before, providing a neat antidote to the temptingly affordable models we've already looked at.

The BMW X3, in particular, has been a runaway success, echoing the qualities and appeal of its X5 big brother, albeit in a more compact package. It's expensive for its size, it's not terrific off-road (despite boasting greater ground clearance than a Freelander) and it's arguably not the most handsome soft-roader ever to hit the streets. But with the aspirational appeal of the BMW badge in its favour, not to mention a range of gloriously smooth six-cylinder engines and fantastic build quality throughout, the X3 is a premium product that deserves its impressive sales success.

And the Nissan Murano? This has to be the most adventurously styled soft-roader to date, which means potential buyers will either love or loathe its looks. Front-wheel drive in normal use, the Murano automatically switches to 4x4 when the need arises – and that might be sooner than you think, thanks to its 234bhp 3.5-litre V6 engine, linked to a CVT-style automatic transmission. Its specification reads more like that of an executive saloon, but the Murano is most definitely a soft-roader; and a niche one at that.

OPPOSITE With the X5 proving so successful, it was only a matter of time before BMW launched a more compact 4x4 in the shape of the X3, a premium product that has proved extremely popular *(BMW)*

How things change

Not all 4x4 fans have been celebrating the expansion of the soft-roader market over the years, because it hasn't solely resulted in extra models joining the all-wheel-drive scene. It has, in fact, also meant some much-loved old-style SUVs being usurped and replaced by far softer designs that, when push comes to shove, are drastically less useful out in the wilds.

Typical of such a move was the new-for-2005 Suzuki Grand Vitara, long-awaited replacement for the old-style Grand Vitara. But where fans of traditional SUVs and off-roaders had previously celebrated the GV's separate chassis, part-time four-wheel drive and simple dual-range transfer box, the newcomer arrived with monocoque construction, electronic automatic four-wheel drive

(with manual override) and far more of an 'upmarket soft-roader' approach to its design.

Critics of the previous model's fairly crude on-road behaviour celebrated, while enthusiasts of its go-anywhere approach inevitably mourned its passing – not to mention the fact that the new Grand Vitara was more expensive than its predecessor.

The 4x4 scene has changed dramatically over the years, and continues to do so today. And with soft-roaders selling better than ever, both new and secondhand, it could be argued that buyers are getting exactly what they've always wanted. Whether a soft-roader is the perfect vehicle for you is another matter, and one that should be considered very carefully.

ABOVE LEFT As you'd expect from any new BMW, the X3 was immediately praised for its quality and the standard of its fixtures and fittings; the soft-roader was growing up fast! *(BMW)*

BELOW Where the old-style Grand Vitara was a proper SUV, its replacement of 2005 was more soft-roader in style – an indication of just how much the 4x4 market has evolved *(Suzuki)*

SUVs & executives

Evolution
of the species

The term sports utility vehicle has been imported from the USA and is often mistakenly used to mean just about any 4x4. But, as the previous two chapters have already shown, there's far more to the all-wheel-drive scene than SUVs alone.

Still, it's the SUV concept that appeals most to a large proportion of buyers; and it's the SUV concept that has stood the test of time impressively well, even if today's models are a world away from their fairly crude predecessors.

Arguably, the first European-designed SUV was the revolutionary Range Rover of 1970, a vehicle more upmarket and more car-like in its driving style than any other Land Rover product before it. And yet, despite being remarkably civilised for its time, the original Range Rover was still an incredible off-road machine, an essential ingredient in the SUV scene over the years.

Because that original SUV was an upmarket product (and because so many of today's SUVs carry similarly prestigious aspirations), we're covering both SUVs and executive-class 4x4s in this chapter. There's so much overlap that to try to split the two groups is often difficult.

From that original Range Rover of 1970 to the relatively sophisticated and upmarket models of today, the SUV scene has matured at an impressive rate. Despite the arrival of the crossover and the soft-roader in the intervening years, the SUV is still very much alive and well. In fact, there's more choice around now than ever before, whether you're looking at the new-car market or seeking a secondhand example.

The major expansion of the SUV scene within Europe was largely thanks to Japanese companies back in the 1980s, with new models such as the Mitsubishi Shogun/Pajero, Isuzu Trooper and Suzuki Vitara really bringing the sector alive. The upmarket Mercedes-Benz G-Wagen also found its own niche, while Land Rover expanded the SUV scene still further with the launch of the Discovery in 1989.

The 1990s saw frenzied activity in the SUV sales charts, with the Nissan Terrano II, Ford Maverick, new-shape Jeep Cherokee, Suzuki Jimny and Grand Vitara, Mitsubishi Challenger and Shogun/Pajero Pinin, Kia Sportage and Series II Range Rover being just a small selection of the newcomers joining the club. Every manufacturer with ambition suddenly wanted to jump on the SUV bandwagon.

The good news about such expansion is that there's now a genuine SUV available for all potential buyers, whether that means a highly affordable compact model or something a bit larger and more expensive, and we'll take a look at some of the best-value examples just a little further on.

The SUV scene has never been just about value for money. These days certain entrants such as the Range Rover, top-of-the-range Discoverys, more opulent Shoguns/Pajeros and expensively-badged BMW X5 and Mercedes-Benz M-Class models are seen as aspirational, upmarket and seriously desirable. The SUV has crossed the great divide between agricultural workhorse and luxury car, and there's now no shortage of comforting opulence available to 4x4 fans with hefty bank balances.

OPPOSITE The original-style Range Rover was the first European model to take the 4x4 concept and transform it into an upmarket, aspirational, SUV-style vehicle (*Land Rover*)

LEFT The success of the Range Rover led to further development over the years, with the Series II model of 1994 taking the luxury-4x4 concept a stage further. The newcomer is shown here with a Range Rover Classic from the same year, as well as the original model from 1970 (*Land Rover*)

Cheap and cheerful?

Because the SUV has been around for so long, it means even those purchasers with relatively minuscule budgets can afford to get involved, with elderly examples of the Suzuki Vitara (itself inspired by the even more basic SJ/Samurai range), Daihatsu Sportrak, Lada Niva and old-style Kia Sportage all offering spectacular value at the bottom of the SUV pile these days.

Of that lot, it's the Vitara that has enjoyed the most fanatical following over the years, though this has diminished somewhat as it has got older. Gone are the days when wide-arched, big-wheeled Vitaras were the ultimate things to be seen in on the car park at McDonald's. Happily, this means a basic Vitara can now be yours for very sensible money indeed.

Launched in 1988, this little Suzuki was the first truly trendy small 4x4 to hit the streets, and proved an instant hit. It had longevity too, remaining on sale in some European countries right through to the 21st century. Even now, a three-door short-wheelbase Vitara looks good, while the slightly blander five-door long-wheelbase model boasts added practicality. With a range of petrol and diesel powerplants available (from 1.6-litre upwards), there's a cheap and cheerful Vitara to suit most people.

Combine reliability with fairly low running costs and you've got a tempting bargain-basement package. That the Vitara is also a fine off-roader (especially with all-terrain tyres fitted) is the icing on this particularly affordable cake.

If handsome looks aren't the top priority for your ultra-cheap 4x4, it also pays to consider the original (1996–2003) Kia Sportage, a dull but functional five-door SUV with 2.0-litre petrol power, a dual-range transfer box and reasonable rather than exceptional off-road capabilities. Early examples are now very affordable indeed, yet manage to offer excellent family transport and decent long-term reliability.

But what if the likes of Vitara and Sportage are just too small for your ultra-basic budget? Don't despair, because some of the older SUVs still popular throughout Europe now offer fantastic value for money, too. I'm talking first-generation Mitsubishi Shoguns/Pajeros and Isuzu Troopers, early Land Rover Discoverys and even the odd 1980s Range Rover – all of which can now be picked up for temptingly small sums.

Then there's Vauxhall/Opel's Frontera, available in Series I (1993–98) and Series II (1999–2003) guises and a choice of three-door short-wheelbase or five-door long-wheelbase layouts. The later Fronteras are good value, while the early versions are downright cheap. Be warned, though, that the Series I Frontera always suffered from patchy build quality, a less than perfect reliability record and a tendency to show its age even after a fairly low mileage. Buy as late a

L 474 YNX

Frontera as you can afford, if this ex-Isuzu design really appeals; you certainly can't knock it for value.

There are pitfalls to watch out for, however, when investing in any relatively aged 4x4. A well used old SUV will probably be suffering from rust to a certain extent, though it's important you differentiate between unsightly surface rust and MoT-failing structural corrosion. Although diesel-engined examples of all these models will take high mileages with ease, you still need to satisfy yourself you're looking at a well-maintained, regularly serviced vehicle.

With family-sized SUVs such as those listed above, most have come with petrol engine options over the years, and these are often cheaper to buy on the secondhand market. Ask yourself, though, whether you can really afford the fuel bills of a V8-engined Discovery if you choose that instead of a turbo-diesel version.

Newer **recruits**

Generally speaking, the newer your SUV, the better it will be, both in terms of overall condition and driving style. And that's particularly true of models such as the Shogun/Pajero, where steady development and the launch of various new-generation versions are indicators of major progress. The Series I Shogun/Pajero of 1983–91 was a worthy and successful design in its own right; but if you can afford to buy a newer (1991–2000) Series II version, you'll find it a more powerful, smoother, better-handling, better-looking alternative. The same happened when the original-spec Isuzu Trooper was replaced by its more modern-looking successor of the same name.

Assuming the Discovery-size SUV you can afford is from the 1990s or later, there's an absolute plethora of models from which to choose. One of the best of the 'old school' SUVs has to be the Nissan Terrano II, a model first introduced in 1993 and still going strong a dozen years later. With its separate chassis, dual-range gearing and plenty of low-down torque in diesel guise, the Terrano is a competent and capable off-roader. While it may lack the sophistication or refinement of more modern full-size SUVs, its excellent value for money on today's used market makes it a tempting buy – particularly if you have a heavy caravan or trailer to lug around.

The Terrano II had a sister model for the first few years of its life, in the shape of the first-generation Ford Maverick. Both vehicles were the result of a joint collaboration between Nissan and Ford, although the Blue Oval's product was subsequently dropped due to disappointing sales – leaving the Terrano to go from strength to strength.

Another excellent workhorse from the 1990s was the Series II Land Rover Discovery, launched in 1998 and a major step forward from the then dated Series I. It drove better, its on-road handling was transformed and its more sophisticated suspension set-up was a joy compared with its predecessor's. Best of all was that the Discovery had lost none of its tough-terrain capabilities, remaining king of the off-road SUV crowd throughout its six-year production run.

America's major success story from the 1990s was the European launch of the Jeep Cherokee, subsequently followed by the larger, more expensive Grand Cherokee. The Cherokee, in particular, achieved healthy sales for its maker, Chrysler, and provided British and Japanese opposition with a top-value, great-to-drive product. Its rugged, square styling looked the part on European streets, while its 2.5- and 4.0-litre petrol engines (subsequently joined by a turbo diesel)

were an absolute joy. This wasn't the most refined SUV around, but in terms of image and capabilities it was certainly one of the most tempting at the time – and remains a superb secondhand buy to this day.

Of today's SUVs, the one which has the most traditional layout and specification must be the fairly rare (in Europe) Hyundai Terracan, a square and boxy five-door model with an unpretentious feel and a hard-working nature. Some might call it dated but, for fans of the no-nonsense approach that just about all SUVs once had, the Terracan is an interesting and value-for-money product. It's certainly a welcome antidote to the over-complication of some of its rivals in the SUV sector.

ABOVE America's Jeep marque returned to the UK and other European markets in 1993, with the Cherokee proving an instant hit in the SUV class *(Author)*

BELOW Buying a secondhand Isuzu Trooper? Like so many of its SUV rivals, this model was significantly improved and updated throughout its career *(Isuzu)*

OPPOSITE Like so many of its rivals, the Terrano II was at its best – and most useful – in five-door long-wheelbase form. Later 2.7-litre diesels provided quite reasonable power *(Nissan)*

ABOVE For an old-school SUV, the Nissan Terrano II sold well over a remarkable twelve-year career – proof that old-fashioned values were still important to many buyers *(Nissan)*

A Japanese phenomenon

The worldwide success of the original Mitsubishi Shogun/Pajero led other Japanese companies to exploit the SUV scene to great effect. But it also gave Mitsubishi a determination to expand the breed, hence the arrival of the new Challenger model in 1998.

Using essentially the same front end as the L200 pick-up truck, the Mitsubishi Challenger was a fairly handsome five-door SUV with all the traditional hallmarks necessary: separate chassis, part-time four-wheel drive, a dual-range transfer box, plenty of torque and decent off-road potential. It wasn't the most high-tech SUV ever to appear from Japan, but it was exactly what scores of buyers wanted, for its simplicity and ruggedness.

Within a couple of years, though, the Challenger was being renamed the Shogun/Pajero Sport, to bring its image more in line with the rest of the family. As the Shogun/Pajero itself was being steadily moved further upmarket, so the

Shogun/Pajero Sport filled an ever-widening gap at the bottom of the range.

Creating an SUV from a pick-up truck wasn't unique to Mitsubishi, for Toyota did much the same thing with its Surf, a model which employed the front end, chassis and drivetrain of the hugely successful Hilux truck. Like the Challenger, the Surf was almost agricultural in its specification, yet it proved to be a formidable competitor in the world of the affordable SUV. These days, secondhand buyers in the UK purchase reasonable numbers of 'grey import' Surfs each year, while the Challenger/Sport proves an equally worthy used buy. With superb reliability, a rugged nature and more than adequate off-road capabilities between them, these two Japanese contenders make an interesting alternative to their more mainstream rivals.

In the meantime, while the relatively straightforward Shogun/Pajero Sport was being sold on its traditional appeal, the Shogun/Pajero itself was being redesigned, re-launched and repositioned in the market place. Indeed, by the time the all-new Series III model was unveiled in 2000, it had evolved into a modern, monocoque-constructed, curvaceously styled executive express with more power, improved refinement and better handling than the world had previously seen from Mitsubishi. The company still claimed excellent tough-terrain capabilities for the newcomer, though the off-road fraternity had its doubts; for that all-important on-road use, however, the latest Shogun/Pajero was light years ahead of its

predecessors, and for this sector of the market that was what increasingly mattered.

These days, any 2000-onwards Shogun/Pajero makes a great buy, as Mitsubishi's reputation for reliability and build quality remained intact through what were some financially turbulent years for the company. Whether you choose the model's superb GDI (Gasoline Direct-Injection) petrol engines or one from a range of very powerful and rather impressive turbo diesels, you'll be making a sound decision. The Shogun/Pajero success story lives on.

Small and beautiful?

Not every SUV, of course, is a family-size holdall in the mould of the Discovery or Pajero. In fact, if size isn't particularly important to you, you'll find some tempting and very capable smaller options out there, both new and used.

For a long time, Suzuki has been the biggest name in miniature SUVs, with the original SJ of the 1980s being arguably the first proper example of the breed. And, as mentioned earlier, the subsequent success of the Vitara really brought Suzuki to the forefront of compact SUV design.

These days, one of the best small-model buys has to be the Suzuki Jimny, a diminutive two- or three-door SUV with 1.3-litre 16-valve petrol power and a choice of convertible or hard-top body styles. It's cheap to buy, fun to drive, economical to run – and it also happens to be a surprisingly fine off-roader.

The Jimny has all the qualities of a good old-fashioned SUV, its sturdy separate chassis, dual-range transfer box, fairly good ground clearance and short front and rear overhangs making it ideal for the off-road enthusiast who wants some inexpensive fun. It will be a sad day if something as basic but as effective as the Jimny gets replaced by a more expensive, more sophisticated product.

That's what so often happens, though, with the new-for-2005 Suzuki Grand Vitara being a very different machine from its predecessor of the same name. The good thing is that the pre-2005 Grand Vitaras are now temptingly good-value, traditional, compact SUVs for the used-car buyer. With a choice of short- or long-wheelbase body styles and a good range of engines on offer, most people in the market for a fairly small SUV will find a Grand Vitara to suit. It may not be such a fine on-road machine as a RAV4, but any old-style Grand Vitara will prove a likeable and usable everyday machine, with good off-road performance also easily achieved. Again, it represents some of the best 4x4 value on today's secondhand market.

Suzuki isn't the only manufacturer of small SUVs, though. There's also Mitsubishi with the Shogun/Pajero Pinin, a range of short-wheelbase three-door and longer-wheelbase five-door SUVs that never enjoyed the same kind of popularity in Europe as most of its rivals. My advice would be to forget the short-wheelbase version, as it's neither a great off-roader nor particularly competent at enthusiastic cornering on the road. Better instead to opt for a five-door model, which also boasts a superior four-wheel-drive system that enables the serious driver to select low-ratio gearing and lock the centre differential. It may not have the greatest ground clearance in its class or the most panache as a fashion icon, but the five-door Pinin is a sound buy and a genuinely capable workhorse.

Vehicles such as the Grand Vitara and Shogun/Pajero Pinin are, of course, ideal if you want a relatively new machine for a not-so-great budget. But what can you do if they're simply way too small for your needs? The unlikely answer could come from India in the shape of the TATA Safari, a Discovery-sized SUV for less than the price of a Freelander. And on the used market too, these crude and basic creatures are almost absurdly cheap. But does that mean we'd recommend one?

Well, it depends what you want from your SUV. The TATA is a spacious seven-seater with an ultra-reliable ex-Peugeot turbo-diesel engine, great off-road ability, loads of equipment for the price and an honest, unpretentious nature that almost has appeal. On the other hand, it's appallingly badly built, incredibly sluggish on motorways, desperately unrefined and is generally considered downright ugly. Would I buy one? If I wanted a no-nonsense seven-seater tractor, yes. But for the vast majority of SUV buyers, that's simply not enough.

The executives

While the odd exception like TATA insists on still producing basic and dated SUVs for an ever-decreasing market, most other companies have taken their SUV concept in completely the opposite direction. In fact, nowadays we've got more luxury-spec SUVs and 4x4s on sale in Europe than ever before, and it's a market that has seen impressive growth during the early years of the 21st century.

The most famous of the executive SUVs is, of course, the Range Rover, and three generations on from the model's rapturous reception back in 1970, it's doing better than ever. It's now seen as a worthy luxury car in its own right rather than the slightly quirky, executive 4x4 it once was, and is considered a genuine rival to the most opulent Mercedes-Benz, BMW and Jaguar saloons in the process. What you get for your money is an impressively well-equipped, stunning-looking vehicle that, thanks to Land Rover's dedication to the cause, is still an astonishing off-road machine.

While it's possible to spend an almost limitless amount on a brand new top-of-the-line Range Rover with every option fitted, there are some bargains to be had on the used market. The old-style Range Rover Classic still oozes class and charm, of course, and a late 1980s or early 1990s Vogue now offers great value in good condition. But it's the Classic's successor of 1994, the second generation Range Rover, that's just as much of a tempting buy these days, with falling values transforming this into an absolute used-car bargain.

Perhaps it's the transformation of the Range Rover's younger brother, the Discovery, that has been the most startling in the executive class. The original model of 1989 was an upmarket vehicle but was also very traditional and, dare I suggest, even quite basic in its technology. And today? Two generations on, the Discovery is a far more daring executive machine, complete with up-to-the-minute styling, a modern monocoque construction, sophisticated all-wheel-drive technology, amazing refinement levels for its class and the kind of luxury-car driving style not previously associated with a non-Range Rover product from Solihull.

The Discovery's metamorphosis into such an aspirational luxury machine in 2004 was an obvious and understandable reaction to the success of BMW's X5, Volvo's XC90, Lexus' RX300 and Mercedes-Benz's M-Class, all of which have established themselves as benchmark executive 4x4s during their lifetimes.

Other companies have, of course, wanted a slice of the executive-4x4 pie in more recent times, with the likes of Volkswagen's Touareg and Porsche's Cayenne joining what is becoming a crowded market. And, happily for both German manufacturers, each model has enjoyed serious success, partly as a result of setting new standards of driver appeal in the SUV sector. These days, to be truly successful as an executive machine, an SUV also has to boast a genuinely rewarding driving experience.

Land Rover are among the specialists acutely aware of this, which is why a dynamic, more compact model was added to its luxury-end line-up in 2005 in the shape of the Range Rover Sport. With the option of a supercharged V8 petrol engine producing the best part of 400bhp, it's obvious the company is taking the luxury/performance SUV market more seriously than ever now.

But, you know, an executive-class SUV doesn't automatically have to be a pseudo performance car in order to win admirers, as several companies have discovered over the years. Take current and recent examples of the Toyota Land Cruiser Amazon and Nissan Patrol for the ultimate proof, both of them offering massive power, astonishing towing capabilities, traditional SUV layouts and the kind of invincible driving feel that, despite being rather dated by latest standards, still has a kind of macho appeal. They're big, they're brutish and they mean business. That they're also superb secondhand buys offering long-term reliability and a Tonka Toy-like indestructibility is the best news of all for many buyers. You might not be getting the latest in high-tech SUV design, but you're getting something that will last; and last some more.

Choices, choices...

Despite so many of today's 4x4s falling into other sectors of the all-wheel-drive market, the SUV scene is still a huge one, with an enormous array of different models – both new and used – of all sizes and values to suit an equally wide range of potential buyers. So whether that means spending next to nothing on a well-used Suzuki Vitara or the price of a medium-size mortgage on a brand new Range Rover is up to you; and your bank balance.

As ever, it's important to weigh up your particular requirements and to make sure the SUV you end up with is actually the SUV that suits you best. Don't forget too, that if you're buying secondhand you should follow the advice we've given in Chapter Four if you're to avoid a potentially expensive mistake.

Whatever your final decision, the good-old SUV sector still offers so much to so many, and still represents the most popular part of the 4x4 market. Given the choice available, that's hardly surprising.

The real
workhorses

Off-road
toughness

It's an irony of the 4x4 scene that despite the USA being the world's biggest market for SUVs, that country's products have – with the obvious exception of Jeep – failed to make a massive impact in Europe. Sensibly sized models such as the Jeep Wrangler, Cherokee and Grand Cherokee have sold in reasonable numbers in the UK, Germany and beyond, but America's full-size behemoths (Chevrolet Tahoe, Cadillac Escalade and others of their ilk) have been conspicuous by their absence. Even the Ford Explorer, marketed in Europe over a number of years from the mid-1990s, met with only mediocre sales success, yet was a high-flyer in the States.

So it is with the pick-up scene, too, the most hotly fought part of the workhorse sector, where throughout Europe it's the Japanese manufacturers that rule supreme. Admittedly, a small minority of European buyers do opt for full-scale American SUVs and trucks via specialist importers, but the numbers involved are relatively tiny. There's no doubt about it: when it comes to one-tonne pick-ups, Japan is the biggest success story in just about every market outside the USA.

This chapter will be dealing with the workhorse-end of the 4x4 scene, the kind of vehicles bought for either their load-lugging commercial capabilities or simply their off-road competence. This is the tough and rugged sector that really sorts the men from the boys.

While most of today's SUVs and 4x4s place on-road comfort and driving style way ahead of rough-stuff action in their list of priorities, there is a small sector of the market where it's off-road prowess that matters beyond almost anything else. While such vehicles are perfectly capable of being used every day with minimum inconvenience, they're certainly not the type of 4x4 that tends to be driven by family buyers or the company-car clan.

The most obvious example is Britain's long-lived and still successful Land Rover Defender series, the closest we've got to a modern-day version of the original Series I Land Rover of 1948. The Defender is a tough, rugged piece of kit that's astonishingly capable off-road (even more so when modified slightly) and is available in a choice of short- or long-wheelbase lengths (known as the 90 and 110 respectively) and passenger-carrying or purely commercial derivatives – the latter including vans and both single- and double-cab pick-ups. Throw into the equation a host of special-use derivatives built by Land Rover's Special Vehicles Division and you've got a Defender for just about any action.

Unlike most rough-and-ready 4x4 workhorses past and present, the Defender uses both permanent four-wheel drive and all-coil independent suspension, giving it almost an air of sophistication compared with, say, the all-wheel-drive pick-up market. You can even order a new Defender with electronic traction control if you so wish. But that's where the sophistication stops, for the Defender's Td5 2.5-litre turbo-diesel engine is no match for the best offerings from elsewhere these days; it's a reliable enough old thing, but its power, torque and economy levels are no longer the best around.

If you take into account the Defender's less than perfect build quality, incredibly cramped cabin and somewhat compromised on-road driving style, you've got a hard-working 4x4 but one that certainly won't suit everybody. On the

tempting, with all Defender-style Land Rovers being fitted with coil-sprung suspension since 1983, which means that even a fairly aged Land Rover can be a reliable, durable, off-road workhorse when the need arises – and all for a fraction of the cost of a new or nearly new example.

The closest rival to the Defender in many ways is the all-American Jeep Wrangler, of course – the final incarnation in a long line stretching right back to the legendary Willys Jeep of World War II. Not surprisingly, the pre-2007 Wrangler has nothing in common with the Willys apart from a passing aesthetic resemblance; but if you're expecting a sophisticated or up-to-the-minute product, you're in for a shock.

The Wrangler uses part-time four-wheel drive and beam axles, with hardly any concessions to modern technology. Traction control fails to make it on to the Wrangler's spec sheet, as does generous ground clearance – although very impressive suspension travel helps to make up for the latter deficiency when out in the rough.

In fact, the Wrangler makes an impressive off-road machine, although the fact it's available only

ABOVE America's legendary Jeep Wrangler still has many fans, despite its lack of refinement and its unruly handling by today's standards. What fun, though! *(Author)*

BELOW Despite subtle upgrades in recent years, the Wrangler remained a no-nonsense, straightforward piece of kit – and that's partly why so many fans still adore it. *(DaimlerChrysler)*

other hand, the Defender makes a fantastic 'investment', boasting as it does some of the most competitive residuals of any 4x4 at any price.

Secondhand Defenders make sound buys, but you need to watch out for signs of hard work, abuse and off-road damage if you're to avoid expensive trouble. Pre-Td5 models are also

LEFT No longer available brand new, the good-old hard-working Daihatsu Fourtrak makes a tempting secondhand alternative to the Land Rover Defender *(Daihatsu)*

in petrol-engine guise means it lacks the low-down torque levels provided by a decent diesel. A 2.5-litre straight-six Wrangler is available in some markets, though most now receive just the 4.0-litre version. Combine its strong performance (up to 110mph flat out) with rather old-fashioned handling characteristics and you've got an entertaining drive. Or, in the wrong hands, a downright scary one!

The Wrangler is a real fun machine that also doesn't mind working hard for a living, and if that's what you're after you'll love it, but remember that its combination of appalling ride quality, wayward handling, total lack of refinement and seriously dated driving style means it's not the ultimate 4x4 for everybody.

The dilemma for both Land Rover and Jeep, of course, is that in the 4x4 market of the 21st century, models such as the Defender and the Wrangler are reduced to minority status. The market has moved on and, pick-up fans aside, only a tiny percentage of 4x4 buyers now want a pure workhorse. So while the Defender and Wrangler have continued to sell well in the early years of the new millennium, how do you actually go about replacing them with new models?

It's pretty much a certainty that the Defender and Wrangler replacements of tomorrow will be far more sophisticated, more complicated

machines – and that's something that the hardcore off-road enthusiast will, understandably, mourn. On the other hand, both companies must give the majority of the market what it wants if they are to continue to succeed.

Meanwhile, there's an excellent alternative to both the Defender and the Wrangler still readily available on the used market in the shape of the Daihatsu Fourtrak, a hugely capable vehicle with real off-road ability to counteract its Defender-like on-road drive. Buy one, preferably with no rust problems, and you'll find yourself with one of the most reliable, durable, almost indestructible 4x4s available for sensible money.

Late-model Fourtraks make particularly good buys, their 2.8-litre turbo-diesel four-cylinder engine providing reasonable power, excellent torque levels and superb towing capabilities. Couple that with good ground clearance and suspension travel and you've got a terrific old-fashioned recipe for off-road success.

It's a great shame that the only off-road-style 4x4 being produced by Daihatsu at the time of writing is the latest Terios soft-roader, leaving the good-old hard-working Fourtrak with no real prospect of a replacement. The Fourtrak may be dead and buried, but if you want one of the ultimate 4x4 workhorses you'll be well advised to seriously consider a used example.

Van-tastic

Throughout Europe and beyond, there has traditionally been a steady market for vehicles offering the convenience of a van and the go-anywhere ability of a proper 4x4, with the ubiquitous Land Rover Defender being the most obvious (and most successful) example. As the market has expanded, so other manufacturers have been keen to join the fray.

One of the first to do so successfully was Suzuki in the early 1980s, when van versions of the tiny but capable SJ410 proved a popular buy with budget-conscious farmers and rural dwellers. It was manoeuvrable, economical, tough, reliable – and, like all other SJ models, an excellent off-road machine. It was followed by a commercial version of the subsequent Vitara, which again enjoyed considerable success.

Larger, family-size SUVs and 4x4s have also been transformed into load-lugging vans by their respective manufacturers, with the Isuzu Trooper Commercial and Daihatsu Fourtrak Fieldman being among the first. These were followed by van versions of the Nissan Terrano II, Land Rover Discovery Series I, Land Rover Freelander and others, all offering the same kind of driving characteristics as their passenger versions but with just two seats, no side rear windows and a very useful load area. Eventually the Isuzu Trooper would go on to become available in both three-door short-wheelbase and five-door long-wheelbase guises, just to ensure it wasn't outdone by the opposition.

Mitsubishi took things a step further when for the 2001 model year the company launched a wide spread of 4x4 commercial vehicles in one fell swoop. Suddenly, the highly respected L200 all-wheel-drive pick-up range (which I'll mention further on) was joined by van versions of the Shogun/Pajero Pinin, Shogun/Pajero Sport and even the Shogun/Pajero itself, transforming Mitsubishi's commercial vehicle range from a single model to a complete and comprehensive line-up of 21 variations in an instant.

The new range was, logically enough, known as 4Work – a title that summed up its appeal rather neatly. Why should drivers of commercial vehicles not enjoy the same pleasures and off-road capabilities as those lucky enough to run

top-quality SUVs? The market for all-wheel-drive commercial vehicles may not be vast, but it's a steady one – and it didn't cost Mitsubishi a fortune to enter, given that its new arrivals were all 'panelled-in' versions of existing 4x4s.

Remove the back seat, blank out the rear side windows and make sure there's a nice, flat load area – and that was it! Suddenly you had a hard-working and (in the UK) VAT-reclaimable van on your hands – and a good-looking one, too. In fact, most Mitsubishi 4Work models simply looked like standard SUVs with rear privacy glass fitted, such was the clever disguise of their commercial reality. And the fact that the Shogun/Pajero Pinin and Shogun/Pajero 4Work models were both available in a choice of three-door short-wheelbase or five-door long-wheelbase guises provided a bigger array of 4x4 van offerings than from any other company at the time.

OPPOSITE The longest-lived of all the 4x4 vans is, of course, the British-built Defender, one of the finest ways of carrying goods across the most inhospitable terrain (Land Rover)

ABOVE Van versions of the rugged Daihatsu Fourtrak won many friends over the years, such was their ability to thrive on hard work and abuse (Author)

MIDDLE LEFT Mitsubishi's range of 4x4 vans is wider than that of any other company, incorporating as it does the Shogun/Pajero, Sport and Pinin ranges – with a choice of wheelbase lengths, too. Shown here is a short-wheelbase Shogun version (Mitsubishi)

LEFT The popular Isuzu Trooper Commercial ended up being available in both short- and long-wheelbase forms to widen its appeal among 4x4 van buyers (Isuzu)

Pick-up a
workhorse

Inevitably, when it comes to 4x4 commercials, it's the pick-up sector of the market that still achieves the biggest sales. In the UK in particular, sales of double-cab one-tonne trucks have escalated at an impressive rate over the past few years, partly because of changes to VAT and company-car tax rules and partly because the products themselves have improved immensely.

For many years, one of Europe's best-selling pick-ups has been the Mitsubishi L200, though this now faces tough competition from the Ford Ranger, Isuzu Rodeo, Mazda B-series, Nissan Pick-Up and the latest Toyota Hilux, all of which also sell in impressive numbers. Slower-selling rivals that are still worth considering include the SsangYong Sports Pick-Up and the Indian-built TATA TL.

Not all one-tonne pick-ups come with four-wheel drive, as most also offer rear-drive versions (often the entry-level models) for those buyers who don't need any kind of off-road capabilities. It's important to make this distinction and to ensure you're comparing like with like when looking at what's available for your budget.

You also need to consider whether you need a single- or a double-cab truck, the former often featuring just a single bench seat and the latter usually offering accommodation for up to five adults. The downside with any double-cab, of course, is the drastic reduction in the length of the load area, although overall payload usually remains the same at around one tonne. Do you need the maximum load length for your money, or will you be wanting accommodation for the whole family? It's your call.

Some manufacturers also offer a compromise-type of cab design, whereby it's a two-door but with enough extra depth for either an interior storage area or even an occasional back seat. They're a reasonable 'halfway house', though very much in the minority sales-wise.

If serious off-road antics are what you'll be expecting your all-wheel-drive pick-up to perform, there are a few points to bear in mind. You see, while most models offer part-time four-wheel drive and a dual-range transfer box (pretty much like any good old-fashioned 4x4 or SUV), the very nature of their design means they also have lengthy rear overhangs in order to maximise load area. As anybody who's been off-roading will appreciate, big overhangs can restrict your action, even if the pick-up's ground clearance is actually very generous. On the other hand, most models offer decent suspension articulation, which means progress needn't be too inhibited.

Another thing to bear in mind when it comes to buying a secondhand truck is that the vast

majority until fairly recently used the (effective, but dated by SUV standards) idea of rear leaf springs. If they opted for a coil-sprung set-up, they'd almost certainly lose out on carrying capacity – and as every double-cab pick-up needs to be capable of hauling a full tonne around in order to comply with the UK's VAT and company-car tax rules, that would be a bad move. So leaf springs are what you'll find under the rear of most used trucks, which means that if you're expecting ride quality and on-road handling to match those of the Land Rover Discovery 3, you'll be sorely disappointed.

In fact, no matter how sophisticated or well-equipped most of today's 4x4 pick-ups appear at first glance, the driving experience is a more agricultural affair. Far from unpleasant, you understand; but definitely less civilised than the best SUVs have to offer.

You do get a lot of vehicle for your money, though – particularly if you're a VAT-registered British buyer and can claim back 17.5 per cent of the all-in purchase price. The most expensive of today's trucks are exceptionally well equipped and make excellent family transport, if that's what you're after. That they're still sturdy workhorses at heart, capable of performing a genuinely useful commercial role, is even better news.

Most manufacturers these days try to market their one-tonne trucks as 'lifestyle' machines, with the most upmarket offering all the accessories and gizmos you could reasonably expect. And if that's your kind of thing, you'll find models such as the Mitsubishi Warrior and Nissan Navara exactly what you're looking for, but before you get carried away, take a long hard look at your requirements and ask yourself whether you actually need all those goodies. If you don't, you could save a considerable sum by opting for a more down-to-earth variant.

ABOVE Some five-seater double-cab trucks are relatively luxurious these days! *(Isuzu)*

BELOW The Izuzu Rodeo (like its many rivals) comes in a variety of trim levels to suit all buyers. Shown here is the Denver version *(Isuzu)*

Buying **used**

Buying a secondhand pick-up isn't dissimilar to buying a used SUV or 4x4, so I won't waste space repeating myself here; much of the information you'll need is already contained in Chapter Four. However, the issue of wear and tear is of particular importance.

On the used market, you'll find some double-cab trucks that have been exceptionally well looked after, essentially used for private-style work. But you'll find far more trucks of all types that have also been used, abused and thrashed almost to extinction, and these are the ones you need to beware of.

It would be unrealistic to expect a three-, five- or seven-year old pick-up to be immaculate throughout, so you can assume there'll be plenty of scratches, dents and minor damage in the load area itself. However, the state of the rest of the vehicle will give a good indication of just how well

it's been looked after, including the condition of its outer panels, its interior and – most important of all – the completeness or otherwise of its service history.

Most of the successful pick-ups of recent years make great used buys when they're in good order, and your final choice will often simply come down to availability on the secondhand market. With the obvious exception of any TATA truck (which, although robust and extremely reliable, are renowned for being basic and workmanlike to drive), most one-tonne offerings are also pleasant enough to drive and easy to live with.

They're also arguably the most useful way to invest in any 4x4, new or used, so it's little wonder the 4x4 pick-up has evolved into as much of a style icon as a workhorse in recent years. Those who've already discovered the genre often wouldn't be seen driving anything else.

ABOVE Not all pick-ups are trend-setting 'lifestyle' vehicles. Indian-built TATA trucks are cheap and reliable, but far less refined and less pleasant to drive than their Japanese opposition. Your choice depends on your own set of priorities *(TATA)*

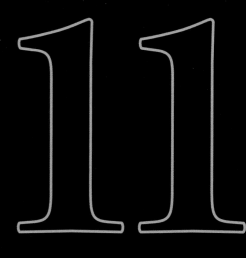

Add-ons
& upgrades

Going **off-road**

For many owners, the concept of modifying or upgrading their 4x4 is completely alien; they're quite happy with their vehicle the way its manufacturer intended, so why bother changing anything? Put simply, it depends on your priorities, your intended usage and, of course, your available budget. To use most of today's reasonably priced 4x4s for nothing more challenging than a shopping trip, the daily school run or the occasional weekend away, there's little point in considering any major modifications. But many owners and enthusiasts now demand more from their 4x4s, with an increasingly large proportion wanting to exploit and improve upon what off-road capability is already there, and just as many are keen to alter and personalise their vehicle's aesthetics; the choice is yours. Let's start with a few suggestions for off-road enhancements…

Not every 4x4 was created primarily as an off-road machine, with models such as the Toyota RAV4 and Honda HR-V being very much 'tarmac transport' first and foremost. They'll get you along a reasonably rough track or across a wet field without too much difficulty, but don't expect them to perform admirably at an official off-road venue.

It's important therefore, to ensure that your 4x4 is worth upgrading; in other words, is there any point investing in tough-terrain tyres and other off-road essentials when the donor vehicle in question is plainly not suited to that kind of work? Better instead to choose a 4x4 in the first place that has a good level of off-road capability already designed in and to then build upon it. Chapters seven to ten have looked at the off-road capabilities of specific models, which should help a great deal when making your all-important decision.

So assuming you'd like your 4x4 to be able to cope with the rough stuff when the need arises, how much work do you need to carry out in the way of modifications? Well, how far you go with any mods depends on how much time and money you want to invest in the project, as well as how seriously you're likely to take your off-roading.

Rest assured that many completely standard 4x4s – including most Suzukis and just about every Land Rover, plus all the Troopers, Terranos, Fourtraks, Shoguns, Pajeros, Patrols, Fronteras and Land Cruisers of this world – are all perfectly capable of getting you through some reasonably tough terrain. In fact, there's absolutely no reason why you shouldn't take most (preferably short-wheelbase) reasonably tough 4x4s off-road and have a lot of fun, without carrying out any modifications whatsoever. But if you're likely to be off-roading on a regular basis, some basic changes are certainly advisable.

For a start, have a look at the tyres on your 4x4 – a subject we've already taken a look at in Chapter Three. Are they the standard road tyres you'll find on most of today's models? If so, they're likely to prove less than perfect in off-road conditions. You need maximum grip, and a standard set of rubber just isn't up to the job. Talk to some of the 4x4 specialist companies we've listed in the appendix and ask them what the optimum choice of tyre is for your model. As we've already suggested, tell them how much of your driving is likely to be off-road and what kind of a budget you have to play with. They'll then be able to come up with the ideal compromise for your needs. Get the right set of rubber on your vehicle and you'll be amazed at the difference in grip and go-anywhere capabilities.

Off-road tyres will certainly get you places you couldn't have reached beforehand, but you don't want to ruin your engine getting there, so an engine snorkel of some description is advisable for serious off-roading. This ensures that the air intake for your vehicle is higher than any water you're likely to be wading through, which is handy when it comes to preventing your engine from seizing up! This is why you will see lots of off-roaders (particularly Land Rover Defenders and Suzuki SJs) with snorkels running up the side of their windscreens – though whether you'll be happy cutting a hole in one of your front wings for the snorkel to exit through is another matter.

OPPOSITE Don't ignore any obvious signs when off-roading; they're there for your own good! Water can do untold damage if your vehicle isn't properly prepared *(Author)*

FAR LEFT If you want to protect your 4x4's interior when off-roading or carrying out any dirty duties, most specialists will be able to supply a set of protective waterproof seat covers for your make and model *(Author)*

BELOW Sealing your 4x4's electrics and fitting a waterproof distributor cap can make for more reliable off-roading and less hassle when heading through deep water *(Author)*

OPPOSITE If you're heading off-road on a regular basis, you'll be well advised to fit an engine snorkel. They are available for most of the popular off-roaders, though many enthusiasts prefer to make their own *(Author)*

RIGHT Heading off-road? Make sure you go fully prepared. A secondhand ex-army shovel, for example, can be particularly useful if you get stuck! *(Author)*

RIGHT Fitting a good-quality electric winch is a great idea for the serious off-road enthusiast, enabling you to haul yourself out of trouble when the need arises *(David Bowyer's Off-Road Centre)*

RIGHT If you're intending to go off-road regularly, have you considered some kind of suspension upgrade? Whether that means heavy-duty struts, uprated leaf springs or even a full suspension lift, the results can be well worthwhile – albeit at a price *(Kayaba)*

You might even want to start thinking along the lines of modified suspension – particularly if your 4x4 has a conventional and easily upgraded leaf-spring or coil-spring set-up rather than anything more high-tech or over-complicated. This involves more expenditure than a set of off-road tyres; but for the benefits gained, it can be worthwhile, and not just when off-roading. Invest in a set of uprated leaf springs from a company such as Milner Off Road, for example, and you'll have a more robust off-roader on your hands, as well as a vehicle even more capable when towing a heavy trailer, caravan or horsebox.

Milner and other specialists are also able to supply uprated shock absorbers, which can again improve the off-road experience – even if there is a risk of a harsher on-road ride. LA Supertrux (and other companies) will even supply suspension lift kits for a wide range of different 4x4s, and although this may sound like an expensive option, for an extra 40mm or so of

While you're at it, sealing your electrical system is also advisable, with a waterproof distributor cap and plug leads being particularly useful in very tough conditions. For most owners, it's not that important; but for the avid off-roader, it's worth considering.

If all this sounds rather 'over the top', it's probably because you're not the kind of owner who will be off-roading in any serious way on a regular basis. On the other hand, why not make the most of what capabilities your vehicle already has, and improve them just a tad? You might then find you're tempted to go off-road in a way that had never occurred to you before.

ground clearance (important for the serious off-roaders) it could be money well spent. Do remember, though, that a suspension lift kit fitted to any 4x4 will affect the on-road driving experience, so you need to decide what's most relevant to your needs: extra clearance for tough-terrain challenges or a first class on-road drive?

Whatever your off-road requirements, take a look at some of the various websites featured in the appendix and see what's on offer from the many 4x4 specialists we've listed. Always think of your particular needs and expectations, and don't hesitate to ask specialists for advice; they're there to help, and most of them are only too willing to pass on their expertise to a genuine customer. Remember that it's your money you're spending – and whatever amount you set aside for off-road modifications won't all be recouped when you come to sell your vehicle. If you're only a very occasional off-roader, is it really worth spending so much to transform your 4x4 into a jungle warrior? Maybe, but it's your call.

Before heading off-road, of course, don't forget to stock up on essentials to get yourself away from trouble when you're out 'in the rough'. At the very least, you'll need some decent boots, a pair of gloves, wheel-changing equipment, a good quality tow rope, some spare petrol, a full water container and a basic tool kit that includes spare fuses, wire, bulbs, a can of WD40 and so on. Failing to prepare yourself in such a way is foolhardy, to say the least. When off-roading in a group or taking part in a 4x4 fun day, there's usually plenty of help around from other willing volunteers; but don't assume there'll always be someone else with a tow rope or a tool kit you can use.

One final point about equipment: many off-road enthusiasts are now fitting electric front winches to their vehicles, an excellent idea if you're going to be off-roading most weekends and likely to be pushing your 4x4 to the limit. Being able to winch yourself up a crazily steep incline or out of a mud bath that proved more than a match for your vehicle can be both useful and pretty good fun. It makes you more self-sufficient too, should there be a lack of help about. Do shop around, and talk to 4x4 specialists about the ideal winch for your needs; prices and specifications vary greatly, with companies such as Warn offering a wide range of winches to suit most pockets. Do your homework thoroughly; you might just avoid spending more money than you need to.

Back on
dry land

If the first part of this chapter doesn't seem to apply particularly to you, that's because you're not an off-road addict – and there's no shame in that. Just because you own a 4x4 doesn't mean you have to head for the hills or find yourself wading through mud at the first opportunity. On the other hand, using a 4x4 primarily for on-road use doesn't mean your vehicle won't benefit from some modifications. And it all starts with aesthetics.

Whichever model of 4x4 you own – from the most humble Suzuki Jimny to the most opulent Mercedes-Benz M-Class – there's no shortage of extras and accessories on the market to make it look a whole lot better. Before you start reaching for your credit card, have a serious think about what you're trying to achieve. Are you after a smarter, smoother on-road look? Do you want to make your 4x4 look a tad more rugged? Or perhaps you're simply after some extra luxury and a more upmarket feel? Think which of these applies to you, because what you spend your hard-earned cash on will vary depending on your answer.

One area that's popular for 4x4 upgrades is that of lighting, with many on- and off-road drivers choosing to boost the lighting of their vehicles using aftermarket spot lamps, fog lamps and the like. Extra front-mounted spots can make a difference when driving anywhere remote in less than perfect conditions. But it's also worth thinking about a rear-mounted, fully directional lamp – particularly useful if you regularly tow a trailer or caravan as you can use the extra lighting to make hitching and unhitching in the dark a lot easier. Just a thought.

OPPOSITE A rear-mounted swivelling spot-lamp like this can be a real advantage when trying to hitch a trailer or caravan in the dark. A very sensible purchase! *(Author)*

FAR LEFT Upgrading the lighting on your 4x4 can be useful, whether or not it's ever driven off-road. These smart Wipac spot-lamps are designed specifically for 4x4 use *(Author)*

LEFT A set of mesh light guards could protect your headlamps from stones and flying debris in any severe off-road situation *(Author)*

Bargain breakers

Before we talk more specifically about what's available, do bear in mind there's an increasing number of specialist 4x4 breakers in the UK these days, offering good quality used parts for all marques. Again, take a look at the appendix for details of some of the best-known 4x4 dismantlers. These are the companies that buy accident-damaged cars, trucks and 4x4s, strip them for spares and then sell off whatever is of value – and they can be a great source of accessories and upgrades. If you happen to own a Japanese 4x4, you're even luckier, as there are breakers specialising in just such vehicles.

One word of warning (which should be common sense but I'll mention it anyway) concerns safety. Under no circumstances should you ever consider buying any used items that are critical to the safety of your 4x4 when the donor vehicle has been involved in an accident. Don't be tempted to cut corners and fit a set of secondhand shock absorbers, tyres or steering components (just three of the most obvious examples) from a write-off when the future performance of such items may well have been compromised by the impact.

Where breakers can be extremely useful, though, is when it comes to upgrades and

accessories. You fancy a front bull bar for your 4x4? It will be cheaper to buy a used example from a breaker; it might need repainting if it's been around for a few years, but the money you save should make that worthwhile. You want to replace your basic 4x4's interior with a donor set from a more upmarket version? Again, get in touch with some of the specialist breakers and you might be surprised at just what's available. Take a look.

BELOW Buying secondhand parts from a 4x4 breaker – or even from a 4x4 show like this – is a good idea, although you need to apply plenty of common sense *(Author)*

Cool new look

Enhancing the appearance and styling of your 4x4 purely for road use isn't rocket science – and it can be great fun, too. Among the most popular choice of upgrades is often a replacement set of alloy wheels, with a bewildering variety of different styles on the market. Your final choice will invariably be decided by a combination of aesthetic preference and what you're willing to spend. Always remember that alloys require more maintenance than standard steel wheels, and are also more susceptible to damage; so if you regularly go off-road or your 4x4 is often used for towing a horsebox through seriously muddy fields, is a shiny new set of alloys likely to be the wisest of investments?

For 'street' use, other popular upgrades include alloy side steps, chrome-effect spare wheel covers and, of course, front bull bars or A-bars.

The subject of bull bars has caused controversy since the mid-1990s, when the issue of pedestrian safety really started to rear its head. Claims were made in the press that any pedestrian struck by a large 4x4 with a bull bar fitted was likely to suffer far greater injuries or was more likely to be killed than somebody hit by a 'normal' car. And to a great extent, this is the current situation.

The fact is that bull bars are still legal in the UK and are a popular 4x4 fashion accessory. Many owners cite their usefulness as a reason for fitting them, too; the inevitable car park knocks that seem to be a part of modern-day driving are, they argue, less of a problem when your 4x4 has an enormous bull bar adorning its front end. And, yes, that certainly makes some sense.

So … will you be fitting bull bars to your 4x4? It's your decision, and I'm not here to influence you either way. If pedestrian safety is of major concern to you, it's worth looking into the availability of some of the more pedestrian-friendly A-bars that are now available through specialists. But if a bull bar is top of your list of requirements … well, there's no denying they do look good. They give almost any 4x4 a certain 'attitude', particularly when they have a chrome finish. Decisions, decisions…

LEFT How do you feel about bull bars and A-bars? Opinions are divided, although a chrome A-bar like this can look superb on the right vehicle *(Author)*

Pick-up **extras**

Owners of one-tonne 4x4 trucks are particularly well catered for when it comes to accessories and upgrades, and it's not unusual now to see a double-cab truck adorned with stainless steel side bars and a bull bar, chromed wheels, extra lighting and all manner of 'bling' aimed at making it stand out from the crowd. Such goodies are generally aimed at owners who use their trucks for non-commercial work, hence the success of the 'lifestyle' variants in most model ranges.

If that's the kind of thing you're into, before you rush out and buy a fairly basic truck only to start ordering lots of goodies, add-ons and accessories for it, ask yourself whether it would be more sensible and less expensive to buy a 'lifestyle' version instead – with all its 'extras' already in place. Models such as Mitsubishi's L200 Animal Cab, Nissan's Navara and Isuzu's Rodeo Denver Max have all been so popular in recent years that there's usually no shortage of examples available on today's used market.

One thing that a huge proportion of 4x4 truck owners also insist on buying, of course, is a glassfibre hard-top, a useful item that transforms your pick-up into more of a van as soon as it's fitted. It means the whole load area is suddenly dry and more secure, while also giving your vehicle an almost SUV-like look.

Check out some of the hard-top suppliers

and manufacturers listed in the appendix for further information. The best news of all is that just about every popular one-tonne truck sold in Europe has at least one hard-top design available for it – and usually a far wider choice than that. Your only difficulty will be deciding which style and specification to go for.

Hard-tops for trucks are usually available from franchised dealers, so check out your manufacturer's official accessories and options lists to see what's around. But with so many independent 4x4 and pick-up specialists throughout Europe these days, the availability is far wider than that – which means competitive prices and some superb products. Take a look at the websites of some of the hard-top makers out there for an idea of exactly what's available – and at what price – for your make and model of pick-up. I think you'll be very impressed.

ABOVE Aftermarket hard-tops are among the most popular pick-up accessories now available *(Mitsubishi)*

Extra **power**

Seriously boosting the power of your 4x4 is an interesting subject area, albeit one that should be approached with caution. Most owners of conventional 4x4s – and particularly those who choose diesel-powered versions – aren't renowned for having tarmac-burning performance at the top of their list of requirements.

Those who do need strong on-road performance will often opt for petrol power, even in a full-size 4x4 with a hefty fuel consumption. And I do mean hefty: compare the fuel consumption figures for a Land Rover Discovery V8 with those for a turbo-diesel version and you'll see what I mean.

On the other hand, you might be lucky enough to find a petrol-powered Shogun, Pajero, Discovery, Range Rover, Land Cruiser, Patrol, or whatever, that has already had an LPG conversion carried out, effectively reducing your petrol bill by as much as half without drastically affecting the performance. You can have just about any petrol-powered 4x4 converted to LPG, but don't expect a professional job on anything bigger than a four-cylinder engine to be cheap; and unless you're intent on keeping your vehicle indefinitely or you cover a huge annual mileage, you need to ask yourself whether such an investment is actually worthwhile.

Turbo-diesel 4x4s of just about any description can be improved upon, of course – but much depends on your priorities. For the biggest boost in performance without sacrificing the long-term reliability of your 4x4, it might be worth investing in something like a Tunit – a relatively simple device that boosts the power of a diesel engine by up to 30 per cent. Produced and sold direct by UK-based Bromleys, Tunits are available for a wide range of turbo-diesel 4x4s these days. Extra applications are continually being added to the range, so contact Bromleys direct to find out the latest information.

The figures speak for themselves. Claims made for Mitsubishi Shoguns fitted with Tunits, for example, are impressive: a 3.2-litre Shogun DI-D is said to have its power boosted from 160bhp to 180bhp, while torque is increased from 276lb ft to a massive 307lb ft. Similarly, a 2001-model Mitsubishi L200 2.5 TD pick-up is said to see power increased to 120bhp (from just 100bhp), with torque boosted significantly from 178lb ft to 207lb ft. Not only does the extra power prove useful out on the streel, but such a noticeable gain in torque also comes into its own when off-roading.

The cost of a Tunit varies from model to model, but I think it can be considered a small price to pay for such a useful boost.

In the UK, it's also worth speaking with Berkshire-based Van Aaken. These are the guys who manufacture and market the Van Aaken SmartBox, a programmable digital device that claims to accurately alter fuelling and injection timing to give substantial gains in both power and torque. These changes are fully mapped across the load and rpm range to give what Van Aaken describes as '…excellent drivability and control while providing maximum power with minimal smoke'.

With a range of SmartBox (for electronic turbo diesels) and SmartPower (for mechanical turbo diesels) add-ons now available, Van Aaken can take just about any diesel-powered 4x4 and give it some vital extra 'oomph', both in bhp and torque. This results in diesel-powered machines with more 'drivability' – more power and torque, fewer gear changes and a generally superior driving experience.

If you don't want to go that far but you do want to make the most of what your all-wheel drive already has, there are some simple options available to you. For example, talk to any 4x4 specialist about the availability of a K&N, Pipercross or Jetex air filter for your vehicle. They offer more effective filtration than a standard filter but, thanks to their enhanced airflow, they also provide a useful (albeit slight) increase in power output, as well as improved fuel consumption.

However you modify your 4x4 to improve its performance, the vehicle will only ever be as good as the sum of its parts – which means there's little point spending money on power upgrades if the engine has already covered a quarter of a million miles and the turbocharger is showing serious signs of old age. Be sensible in your expectations, and only seek an effective improvement to any aspect of your vehicle's performance if it's already a healthy and well-maintained example.

How far do you go?

Whatever the reason for modifying your 4x4, and no matter what you're trying to achieve at the end of it all, the best advice is to keep a firm grasp on reality at all times. With a credit card in your hand and an accessories catalogue or website in front of you, it's very easy to get carried away and spend a not-so-small fortune on add-ons and improvements for your vehicle.

But how much of the stuff do you actually need? And if you're about to spend a sizeable sum on improving the performance and handling of an old vehicle, would you be better off – and have an easier life – if you simply bought a more powerful, newer model instead?

These are all personal decisions, and just how far you go with modifying your 4x4 is down to you. Just remember that whatever you spend on improvements won't add anywhere near the same amount to the value of your vehicle. Make sure you invest only in upgrades that are going to be genuinely useful to you, and you won't go far wrong.

OPPOSITE You want to make your diesel-powered 4x4 or SUV that bit quicker? Aftermarket performance boosts are available for most popular models, including the Shogun/Pajero (Mitsubishi)

INSET OPPOSITE Most of today's turbo-diesel 4x4s can get a power and performance boost via the experts at Van Aaken – without spending a fortune, too (Van Aaken)

BELOW Just how far do you go in your quest for a new, improved version of your 4x4? It depends on your usage, your budget and your requirements. The best advice? Whatever you do, have fun. Your 4x4 is there to be enjoyed (Author)

Specialists, clubs & contacts

GENERAL 4x4 SPECIALISTS (SPARES & ACCESSORIES)

4Site 4x4 Tyre Centres
Tel: 0870 900 9444
Website: www.4site4x4.co.uk
National network of companies specialising in all types of tyres specifically for 4x4s. Call or look online for details of your nearest specialist.

4x4 Accessories & Tyres
Mercury Park, Leeming Bar Industrial Estate, Leeming Bar, North Yorkshire DL7 9UN
Tel: 01677 425555
Fax: 01677 425666
Email: sales@4x4accessoriesandtyres.com
Website: www.4x4accessoriesandtyres.com
Suppliers of general 4x4 accessories. Wheels and tyres a speciality.

Auto Styling UK
Wednesfield Way Industrial Estate, Well Lane, Wednesfield, Wolverhampton WV11 1XP
Tel: 0845 644 4704
Fax: 0845 644 5014
Email: sales@autostylinguk.com
Suppliers of 4x4 accessories and upgrades.

Bromleys
Leigh St, Chorley, Lancashire PR7 3DS
Tel: 01257 274100.
Website: www.tunit.co.uk
Email: info@tunit.co.uk.
Manufacturers and retailers of the Tunit range of power upgrades for diesel-engined vehicles.

Bronco 4x4
25 Broad Street, Leek, Staffordshire ST13 5NX
Tel: 01538 398555
Fax: 01538 398333
Email: sales@bronco4x4.com
Website: www.bronco4x4.com
Off-road wheel and tyre specialists.

Charlton Recycled Auto Parts
Thriplow Heath, Nr. Duxford, Cambridge
Tel: 01223 832656
Dismantlers of all types of 4x4s including Jeep, Mercedes-Benz and Mitsubishi.

CLN 4x4
78-80 Church Street, Chalvey, Slough, Berkshire SL1 2PE
Tel: 01753 570112
Fax: 01753 570114
Email: info@cln.ltd.uk
Website: www.cln.ltd.uk
Suppliers of 4x4 bull bars, styling accessories and spare wheel covers.

Design-A-Cover
Unit 1, Victoria Business Centre, Neilston Street, Leamington Spa CV31 2AZ
Tel: 0870 750 1144
Website: www.design-a-cover.com
Specialists in customised spare wheel covers to your own design.

Direct 4x4
Tel: 01332 601016
Fax: 01332 743102
Website: www.direct4x4.co.uk
Email: sales@direct4x4.co.uk
Specialists in customised spare-wheel covers and other accessories.

Equicar 4x4
Athena Works, Meadow Lane, Coseley, Nr. Wolverhampton, West Midlands WV14 9NQ
Tel: 01902 882883
Fax: 01902 882855
Email: sales@equicar4x4.co.uk
Website: www.equicar4x4.co.uk
Specialist 4x4 breakers.

Explorer UK
Poplar Park, Cliff Lane, Lymm, Cheshire WA13 0TD
Tel: 01925 757588

Fax: 01925 755146
Email: sales@explorerprocomp.co.uk
Website: www.explorerprocomp.co.uk
Suppliers of suspension kits, replacement springs and damper upgrades.

Formula 4x4
Stafford Road, Stone, Staffordshire ST15 0UN
Tel: 01785 811211
Fax: 01785 817788
Email: info@formula4x4.com
Website: www.formula4x4.com
Suppliers of general 4x4 accessories and upgrades.

George Young Double Cabs
Medomsley Road, Consett, County Durham
Tel: 01207 571112 / 571122
Fax: 01207 571113
Website: www.carryboy.info
Email: mail@double-cabs.co.uk
Importers and retailers of Carryboy hard-tops for all 4x4 pick-ups.

Glassfibre UK
Hangar 5, Long Lane, Throckmorton, Pershore, Worcestershire WR10 2JH
Tel: 01386 555787
Website: www.glassfibresuk.com
Email: glassfibres@btconnect.com
Manufacturers and suppliers of hard-tops for 4x4 pick-ups.

GT 4x4
Vange Park Road, Five Bells, Basildon, Essex.
Tel: 01268 584585
Fax: 01268 550292
Website: www.gtfourxfour.com
Email: sales@gtfourxfour.com
Dismantlers of most 4x4s.

Hardtops Direct
Maurice Gaymer Road, Attleborough, Norfolk N17 2QZ
Tel: 0800 298 8018

Website: www.hardtopsdirect.co.uk
Email: sales@hardtopsdirect.co.uk
Manufacturers and suppliers of hard-tops
for 4x4 pick-ups.

LA Supertrux

18 Lanchester Way, Royal Oak Industrial
Estate, Daventry, Northamptonshire
NN11 5PH. Tel: 01327 705456
Fax: 01327 871786
Website: www.supertrux.com
Suppliers of 4x4 accessories and off-road
modifications.

Milner Off Road

Old Hackney Lane, Matlock,
Derbyshire DE4 2QJ
Tel: 01629 734411
Fax: 01629 733906
Website: www.milneroffroad.com
Email: sales@milneroffroad.com
Specialists in parts and accessories for
Japanese 4x4s; established since 1981.

Mud 4x4

Simpsons Business Centre, Buxton Road,
Hazel Grove, Stockport, Cheshire SK7 6LZ
Tel: 0845 430 1201
Website: www.mud4x4.co.uk
Email: info@mud4x4.co.uk
Bull bars, A-bars, roll bars and other
accessories for all 4x4s.

Pegasus 4x4

Unit 11, Bakers Park, Cater Road,
Bishopsworth, Bristol BS13 7TT
Tel: 0117 964 0640
Website: www.pegasus4x4.com
Email: sales@pegasus4x4.com
Specialists in hard-tops and accessories for all
4x4 pick-ups.

Prestige Autotrim Products

Oak Tree Place, Expressway Business Park,
Rock Ferry, Birkenhead CH42 1NS
Tel: 0151 643 9555
Fax: 0151 643 9634
Website: www.prestigecarhoods.com
Imports and suppliers of new hoods for
soft-top 4x4s.

Road & Trail

Church Road, Leverington, Nr. Wisbech,
Cambridgeshire PE13 5DE
Tel: 01945 465337
Fax: 01945 476421
Email: road.trail@talk21.com
Website: www.roadandtrail4x4.co.uk
Specialist 4x4 breakers.

Scorpion Racing 4x4 Centre

Unit D, The Coppetts Centre, North Circular
Road, London N12 0SH
Tel: 020 8211 4888
Fax: 020 8211 4999
Website: www.scorpion-racing.co.uk
Suppliers of standard and uprated 4x4 parts
and accessories, including suspension and
brake upgrades.

Silverline 4x4

Nelson Lane, Warwick CV34 5JB
Tel: 01926 496668
Fax: 01926 490003
Website: silverline4x4.com
Email: sales@silverlinewheels-tyres.com
Specialists in wheels and tyres for all 4x4s.

Specialist Leisure

Unit C2, Golborne Enterprise Park,
Kidglove Road, Golborne, Warrington,
Cheshire WA3 3GR
Tel: 01942 295183
Website: www.specialist-leisure.co.uk
Email: mail@specialist-leisure.co.uk
Importers and retailers of 4x4 accessories.

Thornton Breakers

755 Thornton Road, Thornton, Bradford,
West Yorkshire BD13 3NW
Tel: 01274 834790
Fax: 01274 831019
Website: www.thorntonbreakers.co.uk
Email: thorntonbreakers@btconnect.com
Dismantlers of most 4x4s.

Van Aaken Developments

Crowthorne Business Centre, Telford Avenue,
Crowthorne, Berkshire RG45 6XA
Tel: 01344 777553
Fax: 01344 777557
Website: www.vanaaken.com
Email: vanaaken@vanaaken.com
Manufacturers and retailers of power upgrade
systems for diesel-engined vehicles.

Warn Winches

Arbil Ltd., Providence Street, Lye, Stourbridge,
West Midlands DY9 8HS
Tel: 01384 895700
Fax: 01384 898645
Website: www.arbil.co.uk
UK importers of American-built Warn
winches and lifting gear.

West Coast Off-Road Centre

Gorsey Lane, Banks, Southport
Tel: 01704 229014
Fax: 01704 232911
Suppliers of Ironman 4x4
suspension upgrades.

SPECIALISTS (IMPORTS, TOWING, ETC.)

BIMTA

British Independent Motor Trade Association,
1st Floor, 14B Chapel Place, Tunbridge Wells,
Kent TN1 1YQ
Tel: 01892 515425
Fax: 01892 515495
Website: www.bimta.co.uk
Email: queries@bimta.org
Trade association for the UK's independent
vehicle import industry. Suppliers of BIMTA
certificates of authentification for imported
vehicles.

National Caravan Council

Catherine House, Victoria Road, Aldershot,
Hampshire GU11 1SS
Tel:01252 318251
Fax: 01252 322596
Website: www.nationalcaravan.co.uk
Email: info@nationalcaravan.co.uk
National body of the caravan industry, also
offering invaluable advice for both experienced
and first-time caravanners.

Protechnical Ltd.

23 Clevedon Road, Nailsea, Bristol BS48 1EW
Tel: 01275 859955
Fax: 01275 859944
Website: www.protech-uk.co.uk
Email: carsales@protech-uk.co.uk
Specialists in SVA preparation and
conversions; also sales of imported Japanese
vehicles.

Towbars Direct

Norbrook Trailers Ltd., Tarporley Road, Whitley,
Warrington, Cheshire WA4 4DS
Tel: 01925 730005
Website: www.towbarsdirect.co.uk
Email: sales@towbarsdirect.co.uk
Suppliers of most makes and specifications
of towbars.

Towsafe

Website: www.towsafe.co.uk
Email: towsafe@hpi.co.uk
HPI's car-and-caravan matching database,
offering easy access to official statistics and
towing capacities.

VOSA

Vehicle and Operator Services Agency,
Berkeley House, Croydon Street,
Bristol BS5 0DA
Tel: 0117 954 3200
Fax: 0117 9543212
Website: www.vosa.gov.uk

Email: enquiries@vosa.gov.uk
Official government body responsible for ESVA testing and legislation. Check out the website for further details of ESVA system.

Witter Towbars
Drome Road, Deeside Industrial Park, Deeside, Flintshire CH5 2NY
Tel: 01244 284500
Fax: 01244 284577
Website: www.witter-towbars.co.uk
Email: sales@witter-towbars.co.uk
Manufacturers of towbars for all types of vehicles; check website for nearest retailer.

LAND ROVER SPECIALISTS

AJD Land Rovers
Unit 5, Meridian Building, Nazeing Glassworks Estate, Nazeing New Road, Broxbourne, Hertfordshire EN10 6SX.   Tel: 01992 445634.
Fax: 01992 445638. Website: www.ajdlandrovers.co.uk.   Email: ajd@ajdlandrovers.demon.co.uk
Sales, servicing and repairs of used Land Rover.

BLRS
Stuart House, 97 Station Road, Erdington, Birmingham B23 6UG
Tel: 0121 373 7425
Fax: 0121 384 7412
Website: www.blrs.co.uk
Email: enquiries@blrs.co.uk
Parts and accessories for Land Rovers and Range Rovers.

Crook Brothers
Blackburn Old Road, Hoghton, Preston, Lancashire PR5 0RX
Tel: 01254 852660
Fax: 01254 853334
Website: www.crookbrothers.co.uk
Email: crookbrothers@btconnect.com
Specialists in ex-Ministry of Defence Land Rovers.

Famous Four Products
Warwick Road, Fairfield Industrial Estate, Louth, Lincolnshire LN11 0YB
Tel: 01507 609444
Website: www.famousfour.co.uk
Email: enquiries@famousfour.co.uk
Parts and accessories for Land Rovers and Range Rovers.

Foley Specialist Vehicles
The Roses, Epping Road, Roydon, Essex CM19 5DD

Tel: 01279 793500
Fax: 01279 793007
Website: www.foleysv.com
Email: sales@foleysv.com
Sales, service, repairs and upgrades for all Land Rover models.

Frog Island 4x4
37C Milton Park, Abingdon, Oxfordshire OX14 4RT
Tel: 01235 832100
Website: www.frogisland4x4.com
Email: general@frogisland4x4.com
Parts and accessories for Land Rovers and Range Rovers.

Hallam Brothers
Hayfield, High Peak, Derbyshire SK22 2EU
Tel: 01663 743266
Website: www.hallambros.co.uk
Email: sales@hallambros.co.uk
Used Land Rover Defenders for sale.

High Peak
Capitol Garage, High Street, Chapel-en-le-Frith, High Peak, Derbyshire SK23 9SS
Tel: 01298 811088
Website: www.highpeak4x4.co.uk
Independent retailer of pre-owned Land Rovers.

Jake Wright
Hilltop, Burley-in-Wharfedale, Ilkley, West Yorkshire LS29 7JW
Tel: 01943 863530
Fax: 01943 864840
Website: www.jakewright.com
Email: info@jakewright.com
Supplier of used Land Rovers, plus parts, accessories and upgrades.

John Craddock
North Street, Bridgtown, Cannock, Staffordshire WS11 0AZ
Tel: 0845 344 4130
Fax: 01543 460 160
Website: www.johncraddockltd.co.uk
Email: general@johncraddockltd.co.uk
Used Land Rovers for sale, plus parts, accessories and upgrades.

Land Rover Centre
Lockwood, Huddersfield HD4 6EL
Tel: 01484 513604
Fax: 01484 545534
Website: www.landrovercentre.com
Email: sales@landrovercentre.com
Used Land Rovers for sale, plus parts, accessories and upgrades.

Liveridge British 4x4
Valley Farm, Valley Road, Earlswood, West Midlands B94 6AA
Tel: 01564 703682 / 703685
Fax: 01564 702389
Website: www.liveridge4x4.com
Email: info@liveridge4x4.com

Marple Road Garage
22 Marple Road, Stockport, Cheshire SK2 5QB
Tel: 0161 483 0343
Website: www.marpleroadgarage.co.uk
Email: marpleroadgarage@btconnect.com
Specialists in used sales of Land Rover Defender.

MM4x4
Droitwich Road, Martin Hussingtree, Worcester WR3 8TE
Tel: 01905 451506
Fax: 01905 755323
Website: www.mm4x4.com
Email: parts@mm-4x4.com
Parts and accessories for Land Rovers and Range Rovers.

Nene Overland
Manor Farm, Ailsworth, Peterborough PE5 7AF
Tel: 01733 380687
Fax: 01733 380338
Website: www.neneoverland.co.uk
Email: sales@neneoverland.co.uk
Used Land Rover sales, plus spares, accessories and vehicle preparation.

Nick Kerner 4-Wheel Drive
Moat Farm, Winkfield Lane, Winkfield, Windsor, Berkshire SL4 4SR
Tel: 01344 885222
Fax: 01344 885100
Website: www.4wheeldrive.uk.com
Email: sales@4wheeldrive.uk.com
Sales, service, repairs and upgrades for all Land Rover models.

Paddock Spares & Accessories
The Cliff, Matlock, Derbyshire DE4 5EW
Tel: 0845 458 4499
Fax: 08454 584498
Website: www.paddockspares.com
Email: sales@paddockspares.com
Parts and accessories for Land Rovers and Range Rovers.

PVH Land Rovers
Ellerbeck Court, Stokesley Industrial Estate, Stokesley, North Yorkshire TS9 5PT
Tel: 01642 713550
Fax: 01642 713660

Website: www.pvhlandrovers.co.uk
Email: info@pvhlandrovers.co.uk
Independent supplier of pre-owned Land
Rovers, plus parts and accessories.

Real Steel

Unit 9, Tomo Industrial Estate, Packet Boat
Lane, Cowley, Middlesex UB8 2JP
Tel: 01895 440505
Fax: 01895 422047
Website: www.realsteel.co.uk
Email: sales@realsteel.co.uk
Parts and upgrades for Land Rovers.

Rimmer Bros.

Triumph House, Sleaford Road, Bracebridge
Heath, Lincoln LN4 2NA
Tel: 01522 568000
Fax: 01522 567600
Website: www.rimmerbros.co.uk
Email: lrsales@rimmerbros.co.uk
Major suppliers of parts, accessories and
upgrades for Land Rovers and Range Rovers.

RJ Land Rovers

The Garage, 1 High Street, Sawtry,
Huntingdon, Cambridgeshire
Tel: 01487 830813
Fax: 01487 832300
Website: www.rjlandrovers.co.uk
Email: rjlandrover@sawtry20.fsnet.co.uk
Independent retailer of pre-owned
Land Rovers.

Simmonites

755 Thornton Road, Thornton,
Bradford BD13 3NW
Tel: 01274 833351 / 834306
Fax: 01274 835117
Website: www.simmonites.co.uk
Parts and accessories for Land Rovers
and Range Rovers.

Steve Parker Land Rovers

Lloyd Street, Whitworth, Rochdale,
Lancashire OL12 8AA
Tel: 01706 854222
Website: www.steve-parker.co.uk
Email: enquiries@steve-parker.co.uk
Parts, accessories, upgrades and
servicing for all Land Rovers.

The 4x4 Store

Unit 5, Kestrel Business Park, Sowton
Industrial Estate, Exeter, Devon EX2 7JS
Tel: 01392 446855 / 445262
Fax: 01392 445311
Website: 4x4store-exeter.co.uk
Email: info@4x4store-exeter.co.uk
Parts and upgrades for Land Rovers.

The Defender Centre

Drayton Mount, Drayton, Belbroughton,
Nr. Stourbridge, West Midlands DY9 0BL
Tel: 01562 730404
Website: www.defendercentre.com
Email: sales@defendercentre.com
Major supplier of pre-owned Land Rover
Defenders.

Turner Engineering

Churchill House, West Park Road, Newchapel,
Lingfield, Surrey RH7 6HT
Tel: 01342 834713
Fax: 01342 834042
Website: www.turner-engineering.co.uk
Email: sales@turner-engineering.co.uk
Independent re-manufacturer of
Land Rover engines.

JAPANESE 4x4 SPECIALISTS

Allan's Vehicle Services

The Yard, Wixenford Farm, Plymstock,
Plymouth PL9 8AA
Tel: 01752 700270
Mobile: 07970 301013
Website: www.allansvehicleservices.co.uk
Email: allan@allansvehicleservices.co.uk
Specialist importers and retailers of used
Japanese 4x4s.

Antrac Motors

Rock Garage, Quakers Yard, Mid Glamorgan
Tel: 01443 410389
Mobile: 07831 838833
Specialist importers and retailers of used
Japanese 4x4s.

Auto Japanese Spares

110 Eastcotes, Tile Hill, Coventry CV4 9AS
Tel: 02476 474848
Fax: 02476 695700
Website: www.autojapspares.co.uk
Email: sales@autojapspares.co.uk
Suppliers of parts and accessories for most
Japanese 4x4s.

Batfa Japan Inc.

Setagaya-ku, Tokyo 154-0017, Japan
Tel: 81 3 3413 8080
Email: info@batfa.com
Exporters of new and used vehicles from
Japan to almost any location.

Bristol Import Centre

83–93 Fishponds Road, Bristol BS5 6PN
Tel: 01179 525955
Website: www.bristolimportcentre.co.uk

Email: sales@bristolimportcentre.co.uk
Specialist importers and retailers of used
Japanese 4x4s.

Far East Services

PO Box 5, Bexley, Kent DA5 2ZZ
Tel: 01322 865400
Fax: 01322 865402
Website: www.importedvehicles.co.uk
Email: manager@importedvehicles.co.uk
Specialists in imports of all makes/models of
used Japanese vehicles.

Japanese 4x4 Spares

Birmingham Motor Parts, 610A Coventry Road,
Smallheath, Birmingham B10 0US
Tel/Fax: 0121 766 6008
Email: sales@japanese4x4spares.co.uk
Website: www.japanese4x4spares.co.uk
Suppliers of new parts for all Japanese 4x4s.

Select 4WD

Tel: 01934 627233
Fax: 01934 413700
Website: www.select4wd.com
Email: sales@select4wd.com
Retail suppliers of new Japanese pick-ups.

Select Imports

Broadmere Garage, Ipswich Road,
Grundisburgh, Suffolk IP13 6TJ
Tel: 01473 738958
Website: www.select-imports.org
Specialist imports of all types of
Japanese 4x4s.

Stuart Spencer Autos

Dudley Port, Tipton, West Midlands DY4 7RG
Tel: 0121 557 7795
Fax: 0121 557 7797
Website: www.ssautos.co.uk
Email: ssautos@fsnet.co.uk
Specialist importers and retailers of used
Japanese 4x4s.

MITSUBISHI 4x4 SPECIALISTS

Diamond Auto Parts

Brookbank Garage, Scotland Road, Carnforth,
Lancashire LA5 9JZ
Tel: 01524 734200
Website: www.diamondautoparts.co.uk
Email: sales@diamondautoparts.co.uk
Suppliers of parts and accessories for all
Mitsubishis

Exceeds.co.uk

2 Vale Road, Northfleet, Kent DA11 8BZ
Tel: 01474 535852
Website: www.exceeds.co.uk

Email: sales@exceeds.co.uk
Specialist importer of used Pajeros,
particularly Exceed model.

Family Cars From Robert Tart

Hoo Garage, Gloucester Road, Tewkesbury,
Gloucester GL20 7DA
Tel: 01684 275566
Fax: 01684 275567
Website: www.familycarsuk.com
Email: sales@familycarsuk.com
Importers and retailers of used Pajeros from
Japan, plus parts and accessories.

Mitsubishi Parts Online

Website: www.mitsubishipartsonline.co.uk
Email: mitsubishiparts@courtandsmith.co.uk
Online suppliers of parts and accessories for
all Pajeros, Shoguns and derivatives.

Worcester Road Motors

Worcester Road, Stourport-on-Severn,
Worcestershire DY13 9AS
Tel: 01299 822239
Fax: 01299 822239
Website: www.worcesterroadmotors.co.uk
Retailers of imported used Pajeros
and Delicas.

SUZUKI 4x4 SPECIALISTS

KAP Suzuki

Beecher Street, Keighley, West Yorkshire
BD21 4AP
Tel: 01535 610840
Mobile: 07870 279606
Email: darrenwilson@beeb.net
Website: www.kapsuzuki4x4.co.uk
Specialists in the design, development and
supply of parts for all Suzuki 4x4s. Modified
vehicles built to order. All models breaking for
spares.

Rubbers Suzuki

Tel: 01323 847116
Mobile: 07799 544141
Website: www.rubbers-suzuki.co.uk
Suspension upgrades and other modifications
for SJs, Samurais and Vitaras.

Suzi Q's

9 Brades Road, Oldbury, Warley, West
Midlands B69 2DP
Tel/Fax: 0121 544 0200
Email: info@suzi-q.co.uk
Website: www.suzi-q.co.uk
Sales of standard and modified Vitaras; large
stocks of parts and accessories; full servicing,
repair and MoT facilities.

AUCTION HOUSES ('GREY' IMPORTS)

A1 Car Auctions

Tel: 02380 839009

Car Auctions UK

Tel: 01332 850309

Durham County Motor Auctions

Tel: 01740 650065

Global Vehicle Imports

Tel: 02380 710022

Japanese Motor Auctions

Tel: 0151 922 5333

Motor Way Car Auctions

Tel: 02380 710022

Overseas International Cars
(Wholesalers)

Tel: 02380 384350

CLUBS & ASSOCIATIONS

101 Forward Control Club & Register
(Land Rover)

www.101club.org.uk

All-Wheel Drive Club

www.awdc.co.uk

All Marques Off Road

Tel: 0116 259 5658

Association of Rover Clubs Ltd

www.the-arc.co.uk

Austin Champ Register

Springfield Farm, Horton, Nr. Chipping
Sodbury BS17 6PE

Austin Gypsy Register

24 Green Close, Sturminster, Newton, Dorset

Camping & Caravanning Club

www.campingandcaravanningclub.co.uk

Caravan Club

www.caravanclub.co.uk

Club Discovery

Tel: 01778 590500

Club Off-Road

www.cluboffroad.co.uk

Daihatsu Owners Club

www.daihatsu-drivers.co.uk

Dakar 4x4 Owners' Site

www.dakar4x4.co.uk

Discovery Owners Club

www.discoveryownersclub.org

Forward Control Register (Land Rover)

Tel: 0191 3712527

Freelander Club

www.freelanderclub.co.uk

Freelander Register

www.freelander.fsworld.co.uk

Frontera Owners Club

www.fronteraowners.co.uk

GLASS (Green Lane Association)

www.glass-uk.org

G-Wagen Owners Association

Tel: 07000 492436

Isuzu Trooper Owners Club (UK)

www.itocuk.co.uk

Japanese 4x4 Club of GB

Email: jap4x4club@yahoo.co.uk

J33P Adventure Club

www.j33p.org

Jeep Club

www.jeepclub.co.uk

Land Cruiser 4x4 Club (Toyota)

Tel: 01793 497366

Land Rover 4x4 Enthusiasts' Club

Tel: 0171 485 8813

Land Rover Series I Club

www.lrsoc.demon.co.uk

Land Rover Series II Club Ltd

www.series2club.co.uk

Land Rover Series III Club

Tel: 01543 423326

Lightweight Land Rover Club

Tel: 0204 396449

Mahindra Register

www.mahindra-register.org

Military Vehicle Trust

PO Box 6, Fleet, Hampshire GU13 9YD

Mitsubishi L200 Owners' Club

www.L200.org.uk

Mitsubishi Owners' Club

www.mitsubishi-cars.co.uk

Mitsubishi Pajero & Shogun
Owners' Club

www.psoc.org.uk

National Niva Owners' Club (Lada)
Tel: 01654 711891

National Off-Road Association
Tel: 01332 811130

Nissan 4x4 Owners' Club UK
www.nissan4x4ownersclub.co.uk

Pajero Owners' Club UK (Mitsubishi)

www.pocuk.com

Pinzgauer Owners' Club
Tel: 01686 413151

Range Rover Register Ltd
www.rrr.co.uk

Rhino Riders (Suzuki Enthusiasts)
www.rhinoridersclub.co.uk

Scottish Land Rover Owners' Club
www.slroc.co.uk

Scottish Off-Road Club
www.sorc.org.uk

Suzuki Rhino Club
Tel: 01892 535110

Toyota Enthusiasts' Club
Tel: 0181 898 0740

Toyota Owners' Club
Tel: 01737 168585

UK Jeep Club
Tel: 01302 534330

UMM Owners Club
Tel/Fax: 0118 941 5327

Vauxhall 4x4 Club
Tel: 01582 734404

OFF-ROAD SITES & ORGANISERS

British Off-Road Driving Association (BORDA)
Tel: 01264 712093
Website: www.borda.org.uk
Email: info@borda.org.uk
If you're tempted to embark upon off-road training or you simply want an off-road experience for a day, log on to the BORDA website for details of your nearest member company and the facilities they offer. All members adhere to a BORDA Code of Practice and offer professional tuition at all levels.

4x4 Funday
The Beeches, Llanidloes, Powys SY18 6EP
Tel: 01686 413151
Fax: 01686 413040
Email: richard@4x4funday.co.uk
Website: www.4x4funday.co.uk
Organisers of non-competitive off-road fun days in Warwickshire, Worcestershire, Shropshire and Lancashire. Typical costs start at £30 per vehicle per day.

Langdale Quest
Bickley Rigg Farm, Bickley, Langdale End, Scarborough, North Yorkshire YO13 0LL
Tel: 01723 882335
Fax: 01723 882375
Email: info@langdalequest.co.uk
Website: www.langdalequest.co.uk
10,000-acre off-road centre, claimed to be the largest of its kind in the UK.

Motor Safari
Unit 230B, Redwither Central, Redwither Business Park, Wrexham LL13 9UE
Tel: 01978 754533
Fax: 01978 754534
Email: info@motor-safari.co.uk
Website: www.motor-safari.co.uk
Off-road adventure driving and green laning at venues throughout the UK.

Sahara Travel
Abbey House, Dublin 1, Ireland
Tel: 00353 1 496 8844
Website: www.saharatravel.com
Specialists in off-road exploration holidays to Northern Africa – Algeria, Libya and Tunisia.

Trailmasters International
Tel: 01691 649194
Email: info@trailmasters.com
Website: www.trailmasters.com
Organisers of overseas off-road safaris and UK-based 4x4 weekends.

Index